My Life Investment Journal

EMPOWERED TO STEP INTO THE NEXT LEVEL

Nicole L. Brown

ISBN: 978-1-957443-11-9
        978-1-957443-12-6 (ebook)

Printed in the United States of America

First printing edition 2023.

JayMedia Publishing
Laurel, MD 20708

www.publishing.jaymediagroup.net

Front cover photograph courtesy of Tiyana Ellis, Tiyana Rashell Photography.

Back cover photograph courtesy of Alisha Nicole Photography.

To my Mom, Pam Hooker

*The greatest encourager, confidant, prayer warrior, and mom
a girl could ever have. I hear your voice of wisdom and miss
your physical presence every day. I am determined to live
my life as I observed you live yours, standing firm in faith
and giving God the glory every step of the way. I dedicate
this labor of love to you as you devoted your life to us.*

TO GOD BE THE GLORY!

Table of Contents

Leadership

Foreword

God promises in Proverbs 4:12, *"That your progress will have no limits"*. Yet many people are stuck, not moving forward, and existing in a world without progression. While some are not willing to put the effort in to do what they know they need to do, others simply don't know what to do. In either scenario, wouldn't it be wonderful to have your very own coach to guide you in making great life choices, especially in areas where you are not sure of yourself? Well, look no further! You have a coach at your fingertips in Nicole Brown's *"My Life Investment Journal — Empowered to Step into the Next Level."*

The Word of God tells us in Proverbs 29:18 (HCSB) *"Without revelation people run wild, but one who listens to instruction will be happy."* In the pages of this journal, you will walk with Nicole as she helps you with DIY guidance in every aspect of your life. You'll discover instructions and answers to questions you didn't know to ask. Within these pages, Nicole has created a judgment-free zone that will provide you with countless opportunities to deep dive into your own thoughts, decisions, and heart intents, plotting where you are in conjunction to your intended destination. The weekly entries will help you to stay on track in your personal journey. In this journal, you'll discover what it takes to make the investment in your own life that will lead you to progress without limits!

Pastor Cynthia Brazelton
Co-founder, Victory Christian Ministries International and Author

∧∧***

Let me tell you a little story. I once started a speech with a barrage of four-letter words, unapologetically bold and audacious. I didn't give a damn about convention or what anyone thought. Later, I discovered that Nicole, the remarkable author of this workbook, was a pastor. Yep, you read that right—a pastor! I felt like I'd just walked through a tornado of profanities in front of Mother Teresa.

I couldn't hit the apology button fast enough. I profusely said I was sorry, fearing I'd offended her beyond repair. But you know what Nicole did? She hugged me and said, "Honey, you be you. I love you for that. I learned a lot. Gifts come in every type of box and wrapping paper. You are how the gift is wrapped." That's when I knew she was the real deal: no judgment, no pretense, just acceptance and love.

Nicole is the kind of person who doesn't sugarcoat a thing. There's no fluff, no filler, in her words. She's all about positive forward movement blended with bold, decisive actions. And let me tell you, that's a rarity in this world.

As you dive into the pages of this journal, remember this: Life isn't about being perfect. It's about the journey, the messy moments, and the beautiful mistakes that shape us. Each week is a new chance to work on yourself, to forgive your blunders, and to learn from your missteps. Embrace the process because that's where the magic happens.

One of the biggest lessons I've learned is that people who judge you don't matter. They're just spectators in the grand arena of your life, casting their opinions from the cheap seats. The ones who truly matter—the ones who'll stand by your side through thick and thin—don't judge you. They celebrate your growth, applaud your resilience, and lift you higher.

So, don't hold back. Dive into this journal with all your heart, knowing that Nicole's wisdom and guidance will be your trusted companions on this journey. It's the kind of journey that leads to an authentic and purposeful life.

Nicole, you've poured your heart and soul into this journal, and I couldn't be prouder to be a part of your journey. Keep being unapologetically you, my friend, and inspiring the rest of us to do the same.

Here's to your incredible growth, audacious authenticity, and the fantastic journey ahead.

With unwavering admiration and love,

Dawnna St Louis
Co-Founder, Fyre Savvy

****

Words cannot express the true impact the life of Nicole L. Brown has had on me and my family. From lives that connected in our early 20s to a present-day life of deeper connection in our 50s, Nicole L. Brown is a true woman of character who is consistent and deeply rooted faith in God. I have witnessed, both close up and on the sidelines, the power that comes from the investment she placed in her life and the love and empathy she pours into the lives of her family and others, time and time again. Inspired by her life and living legacy, I, too, am being transformed, and my family is better for our connection to her.

Words cannot express the true impact the life of Nicole L. Brown has had on me and my family. One thing I know for sure: she is worth your time, her words are worth considering, and her actions are worth imitating.

So, what are you waiting for? Invest in YOUR life...prompted by the words of a woman who can back it up.

Katherine Phillips-Parrish
CEO and Chief Learning Strategist, Phillips Learning Design

****

I am truly honored and excited to introduce you to "My Life Investment Journal" by the incredible Nicole L. Brown, a business coach expert and faith-based leader whose expertise and proven success in the field of business coaching have left an enduring mark on the lives of many, including my own.

In today's fast-paced and often chaotic business world, finding a coach and mentor who can provide professional guidance and a faith-infused perspective is a rare and invaluable discovery. Nicole brings a unique blend of expertise and spirituality to her coaching practice, making her a trusted partner on the journey to personal and professional growth.

Having witnessed Nicole's work firsthand, I can attest to her remarkable ability to inspire and guide individuals toward great success. Her coaching is not just about setting goals; it's about pressing toward those goals, next-level empowerment, and self-discovery. Nicole is not just a business coach but a beacon of light, insight, and guidance. Her unique ability to blend casual, relatable wisdom with a deep well of professional expertise is genuinely remarkable. Through her coaching, she has helped me achieve extraordinary business success and accomplishments as a small business owner.

"My Life Investment Journal — Empowered to Step into the Next Level" is a testament to her commitment to advancing personal and professional

growth with the individuals she works with. Through this journal, you will experience the power of being intentional, self-reflecting, and taking your business to the next level with consistent and proven strategies. Each page offers you an opportunity to invest in your growth and development and your business. With Nicole as your guide, you can be confident that you are learning from one of the best in the field.

As you embark on this journey, I encourage you to embrace it with an open heart and a readiness to explore. This journal is your personal blueprint for self-discovery in your business and life. There are no rigid rules here, no one-size-fits-all approach, but instead, you'll find a safe space to reflect, grow, and nurture your personal and professional goals.

So, here's to your self-investment journey, guided by the expertise and wisdom of Nicole L. Brown!

Nikkimah Davis, LCSW
Safe Routes LLC — Mental Health & Mindset Clinical Counseling, Coaching, Training, and Consultation Services

Acknowledgements

The list of people my heart wants to acknowledge would double the size of this book. I am grateful to so many, and that gratitude is expressed in the pages of this journal as what you gave and taught me is a part of who I am and what has been accomplished in my life. I am forever grateful to you. However, I must mention a few people by name.

Family Tribe

With my heart and soul, thank you, Steve Brown, my amazing husband. Baby, look at us! None of our life would have been possible if not for you. Your unwavering dedication and love for God have stabilized our family in the highs and lows. Thank you for believing in me. To our children Nikki, Steve, Stephanie, and our godson Ricky. You four have poured so much life, joy, love, and laughter into our home. Never a dull moment! Thank you for every "You can do it, Mommy!" When I want to quit, one look at one of you reminds me of why I must keep going. To Frank Hooker, my Dad. You were my first love, the foundation of so much in my life. You taught me to be confident in myself and God. When I was growing up, and the storms of life hit, I knew I could run to my Daddy for comfort, protection, encouragement, and truth. That has shaped my relationship with my Heavenly Father. Thank you. To Nikea Maria, my sister, this generation's most extraordinary vocal artist! I believe in you, too, Kea, I always have, and I always will. I am proud of you and your accomplishments. You, Ryan, and the boys mean the world to me. Frank Hooker, Jr., thank you for always checking on me and for being the life of every party you attend. To my brother Sean Henderson "Hooker" — always top shelf! Angie Henderson, Sean Jr., Kaycee, and Justin — always family. To Papa and GiGi, my grandparents, you shaped and knitted this family together with love and truth; we stand on that today. Thank you both always. Aunt Linda, I can always count on you to show up — thank you. Aunt Carlene, my other mother, thank you; you always made me feel like a queen. To my cousins John, Cameron, TJ, and Donny, we will always stand strong and tight; we don't know how to do it any other way! I have to say I'm grateful for the wives you selected to help me keep you four in check. Paulette, Vickie, Eve, and Trina, thank you so much! My sister Karen Smith-Young, for the past 20 years your unwavering connection to this family has blessed us. I love you. To all of my aunts, uncles, cousins, nieces, nephews, and others, thank you. I love you all.

Sister Tribe

To my sister tribe, my closest friends, my girls... do I keep going? Shanel Evans, Jada Jackson, Carol Jones, Michelle Lewis, Eva Powell, and Sabrina Sanchez, what can I say in a few words to express your value in my life? The laughter, support, tears, disagreements, encouragement, acceptance, love, understanding, and unity between us is not normal, and I love it. It actually fits us because we are far from normal! Thank you for every moment. I love each of you!

Business Tribe

Nakeya Bridgeforth, Kiy Kiy Collazo, Lorraine Driggers, April Edwards, Sherice Griffin, Diamond Harris, Lafary James, Cindy Johnson, Leeana Johnson, Adrienne Jones, Marnie Lacey, Michael Ransom, Gwen Smith, Taiesha Tilghman, and an extremely long list of others, thank you. From the depths of my heart, I am so grateful. Without your heart, passion, talent, dedication, and expertise poured into my visions, dreams, and ideas, there would be no successes and no businesses. At every successful business endeavor, God provided me with a team of professionals so that together, we could accomplish what I could never do alone. Thank you for being an answer to my prayers. I love you all.

Secret Weapons

To Melanie Freeman and Tiffani Horne, my little sisters, my secret weapons, thank you. It seems like you have been a part of my life since forever. As I look back, you are always there covering, encouraging, helping, listening, supporting, cheering, trusting, sharing, laughing, crying, praying, and living life day to day — moment to moment. I have loved the honor of watching you both grow into the amazing women you are today, defeating the giants, breaking the barriers, and walking strong in who God has created. I love you both.

Coaching Tribe

Nicole Allen, Renee Brooks, Nikkimah Davis, Valorie Eaglin, Patricia Fowler, Katherine Parish, Jada Prince, Jessica Robinson, Jackie Sanders, and Cherie Small, thank every one of you! Some of you have been a part of my coaching program from the beginning, and others were a part of our first mansion retreat, and I am grateful for you. Thank you for trusting me, thank you for applying what you have learned, thank you for pushing past the ceilings to the next level, and thank you for growing. You are the best proof that the concepts in my head are working. Your changed lives are often my gentle hug and reminder from God of the value of my purpose. You did it, ladies! And I am proud of you.

Welcome From Coach Nicole

Welcome! With my best cheerleader roar and coach's voice all rolled into one, I want to say I'm so excited that you have decided to invest in yourself! In that investment plan, I am honored that you chose *"My Life Investment Journal — Empowered to Step into the Next Level"* to support your decision. There are many great options to choose from, but here we are together; thank you.

My Life Investment Journal — Empowered to Step into the Next Level is an accumulation of every breath I've breathed, every person I've met, and every tear I've shed. Delicately woven in the pages are the moments I've wanted to quit, the victories I've celebrated, the love that has filled my heart, and the setbacks that caught me off-guard. Within this life work, you will meet the people who stayed, those who left, and the lessons they both taught. This literary work is a portion of my life, presented to empower others to step up into their next level.

I love journals that allow me to read in my order and at my own pace. So, of course, that's what I created. Each section has a journal entry from me, then an opportunity for you to invest in yourself around the discussed subject. Take a week or two per section; you are the captain of this trip. However, do yourself a favor; don't just read the pages. Participate in the investment work: that is where you will discover this journal's most significant advantages and benefits. Regardless of your challenge, remember *you are not alone*, and *don't quit*. Ok, enough chatter, let's get going. This is going to be amazing! See you inside.

With Eager Anticipation

Nicole L. Brown

Your Coach

Self

Give Yourself Grace

I had just ended an incredible, power-packed, whirlwind month that had me moving from one great endeavor to another. A dream trip to Paris, I attended and supported a life-changing retreat of a member of my sister tribe; the next day, I began preparing to host the largest retreat of my career and everything in between. Everything had gone exceptionally well. I had every reason to celebrate.

I was on my way to meet a client, and suddenly, I felt as if I was going to have an emotional breakdown. I pulled over and called a sister; I needed help! Although I had enjoyed over a month of great success, it was also a month of go, go, go. A month of working to ensure that I did not let anyone down. A month of overloading myself and taking care of everyone else. A month later, in retrospect, I realized that I failed to give myself permission to take time to breathe and look after myself. I didn't let others down, but at that moment, on the side of the road, I realized I had let myself down. While I was giving to others, I failed to give myself grace.

I forgot to practice the safety nets I teach others to follow as *The Purple Hair Coach*. I did what I told others not to do. I broke some of my golden rules and was reaping the negative rewards. It was time for the coach to return to training camp!

Rule #1 — *You don't have to do everything. It's ok not to get everything done. Put a cap on your daily list of things to do.*

> Oh, I completely ignored that rule. I did it all from when my feet hit the floor until my head hit the pillow. Everything had to get done, and there was no room for grace. I was my own taskmaster.

Rule #2 — *Don't feel bad for taking time to rest.*

> Yep, I flew right past the rest period. Even though I knew I needed rest, I convinced myself there wasn't time. And if my body said to "rest," I would not submit to the momentary "weakness." The thought of taking a break made me feel guilty with so much to do.

Rule #3 — *Daily do something that you love to do. Don't grind and forget about yourself.*

> As I'm sure you have guessed, I get a big zero there, too. There was no room or time for me. After all, I had so much to do for

others. It was grinding season, and I assured myself there would be time for me later. I didn't even take time between successes to stop and reflect on the greatness that just happened; instead, I charged head-on to the next great work.

I was on the side of the road somewhere between worship and exhaustion. I can't explain the highs I felt from these successful events. Seeing the light in my husband's eyes as he visited places he had dreamed of, watching women step up and begin to walk in their authentic selves, watching women of all walks of life come together, sharing their struggles and victories using both to step up to the next level. The entire time, I was stuffing moments in my mental suitcase with a promise to myself to visit and celebrate the victories later.

As I heard the voice that has comforted and encouraged me for years on the other end of the phone, I recalled that even great successes must be processed correctly. Yes, even the most incredible victories can be a great weight. I knew what I had to do, exactly what I would tell others to do in times like these. I had to shower myself with grace and return to the basics — refocus, reset, and restart.

- **REFOCUS** — I granted myself guiltless permission to stop. In my period of stop, I spent much-needed time investing on the inside. Like a professional photographer re-focuses the camera lens as they move from one scene to another, I refocused my thoughts. I gave way and allowed myself to peel back the layers of the last month. I mentally enjoyed the successes and victories. I breathed in and out. Even for a moment, I allowed a time of gratitude for all God allowed to pass through my hands.

- **RESET** — As a coach, I share with my clients that there are times when you must hit the reset button. Reset allows you to regroup and recharge. In the calmness of the moment, I let my thoughts gently move forward to the big picture of what was next. After refocusing, I could reorganize my thoughts in a way that began to rejuvenate me from the inside out.
- **RESTART** — Your phone and computer will notify you when updates are available. After the updates load into your device, the next thing you must do is restart your device. The restart allows you to receive the fullness of the new features. I believe we all need to hit restart occasionally. Allow the old information to be placed in the proper storage while making room for the new. I had to restart. Not to mention, I had a client waiting for me; there was so much before me. However, I knew my ability to be effective and successful was tied to my grace-filled restart.

Wherever you are in your journey to the next successful endeavor, remember to give yourself grace. You got this.

It's ok not to have it all together all the time.
Give yourself grace. ~ Unknown

Now It's Time To Invest

Is your list of things to do etched in stone, or is flexibility factored into the preparation?

What do you do at the end of the day when you realize the list of things to do is incomplete? How do you feel about leaving things undone? Over the long haul, are your feelings healthy and productive?

Who do you call when you feel overwhelmed? Who calls you when they feel overwhelmed?

On a scale of 1 (the worst) to 10 (the best), how successful are you at giving grace to others? Use the same scale to assess how you are at giving grace to yourself. What do the two ratings reveal to you?

Living in the Now

Recently, Steve, our girls, a family friend, and I were having a late dinner at one of our favorite spots in Virginia. The conversation was light and filled with laughter. We reminisced, caught up on the present, and tossed thoughts about the future. At some point, we noticed that most groups were doing the same — living in the now, enjoying life, and in the moment. Cell phones were not the center of entertainment; taking pleasure in the people at the table was the purpose. Sure, even at our table, occasionally someone picked up a phone, but just as quickly, they put it down, drawn back to what was happening at the table. We were living in the now and loving it. We had formed the habit and created the routine of not allowing the cell phone to abduct us out of the moment.

Typically, when you say the words *habit* or *routine* immediately, a picture of a mundane, blah, or rut of existence is formed in your mind. No one wants that kind of living! Get rid of that mindset right now. I enjoy living life too much to promote anything that will turn my days into blah! Here's what I discovered: developing habits and routines can be fun and power skills that will lead you to tremendous success.

Now, the truth is that <u>not</u> all habits and routines are fun. Honestly, some can be mundane, but they are necessary. For instance, the routine of running or walking outside, for me, is like eating sawdust with no water to chase it down. Don't judge me, and I won't judge you. However, I understand the need for exercise to live healthily, so we created a gym in the basement. Yes, I admit I don't visit the basement enough; we are all working on something, but you get what I'm saying.

As well, not all habits are good for you or your vision. Your habits can either promote or hinder your vision. Occasionally, I look at my habits and consider why I do what I do. Some habits were good in one season, but now they serve me no purpose. I discovered that other practices were holding me back from my purpose. During these times of self-evaluation, I inventory my habits; in other words, I stalk myself to learn my ways. I discovered the routines I wasn't conscious of because I did them in automatic pilot mode. I am determined to cut out of my life any practice that wastes time and holds me back. In some cases, getting rid of the old took tremendous effort, but I was determined to retrain my brain.

It's essential to be mindful and purposeful of your habits and routines; they reflect your priorities. As I consider establishing new habits and routines, I try to filter them through a thought process, "Does this support the success of my vision and goals?" I said try because sometimes I let habits or routines slip in that don't support what I'm doing or where I'm going. We all get sucked into saying yes without considering the true cost of our yes.

Let's talk about this for a moment. I've been there where I've said yes to something that became a part of my routine and later realized, "Oh, Nicole, you should have used your veto power and said no!" However, since I gave my word, I felt stuck dreading every time I had to pour my resources, time, money, energy, creativity, and heart into that thing! It was horrible. However, taking inventory of my habits and routines, I realized I could not hold on to a commitment or routine I needed to let go of. Sometimes, you must let people know that you said yes without thinking. Talking it through can usually lead to a peaceful resolution.

Your habits and routines should promote your desire to live life to the fullest, living in the now! Make it your habit to inventory your habits and routines annually, keeping only those that support your current vision and direction.

I don't think Steve and I have ever told our children to live in the moment by putting those cell phones down. They watch us prioritize them by putting ours down, and we have so much fun living in the now that we aren't interested in tracking what's happening outside of our time. I love our habit of living in the now, living life to its fullest.

Be present, it's the only moment that matters. ~ Unknown

Now It's Time To Invest

This week, your assignment is to stalk yourself. Really think about why you do what you do. Like a private investigator, record notes to remind yourself of your discoveries. List your habits and routines and decide if they are good for you this season. Then, make plans to eliminate the ones that must go. Act on your plan.

Be Your Authentic Self

Your authentic self goes beyond what you do for a living, what possessions you own, or who you are to someone (mom, brother, girlfriend). It's who you are at your deepest core. It is about being true to yourself through your thoughts, words, and actions and having these three areas match each other.

I have seen people allow external influences, such as culture, community, peers, haters, family, and even social media comments from cyber "friends" to change who they are at the core. To be and remain your authentic self, you cannot be moved by external influences to change. You must stay true to your personality, personal values, and the heart and soul of who you are.

I love my sister tribe! We are all so different, and we are not intimidated by each other's authenticity. In fact, we celebrate and embrace our differences. Don't be afraid to be you because you are different. The truth is you ARE different, and you're meant to be different — your authentic self. For you to be an imitation of someone else would rob the world of the real you.

Even in marriage, never lose who you are. Leo Tolstoy said, "When you love someone, you love them as the person they are, and not as you'd like them to be." Steve and I are different, both our own authentic selves, and we celebrate that truth. It's our differences that make us whole. When the Bible speaks of a husband and wife becoming one, the idea is not that the wife becomes a clone of the husband or vice-versa. The picture in marriage is that together, the two become something they could never become apart while never losing their authentic selves.

To be authentic in who you are:

- **OBSERVE YOURSELF.** Honestly, who are you? Deep down inside, who are you? I am not asking who you were taught to be or pretend to be or who you have become to please others. Who is your authentic self? Who is the amazing person behind the mask?
- **DEVELOP COURAGE AND FACE YOUR FEARS.** Are you hiding your authentic self because of fear? Because of what others will think or say? What if I fail at being who I am? What if I'm rejected? Come on, develop courage, and face your fears. The worst thing you can do is continue living a lie by being someone else. A standing ovation for the person you pretend to be is not a standing ovation for your authentic self.
- **LOVE YOURSELF AND HAVE COMPASSION FOR OTHERS**. You will never truly love others until you learn to love yourself, wrinkles, flaws, and all. Being your authentic self will free you to be more compassionate with others. If you are locked inside yourself and consumed with keeping your mask on to hide who you are, how can you come from

behind the mask to allow sympathy to move you to act on behalf of another's suffering? Being critical of your authentic self will make it easier for you to be less critical of others.

- **SPEAK YOUR TRUTH.** Don't allow intimidation to silence you because your truth differs from another. Always let others be who they are and have their own opinion.

- **ASK FOR HELP WHEN YOU NEED IT.** Do you see asking for help as a sign of weakness? Asking for help doesn't weaken you; it speaks to your strength and maturity. Being your authentic self is not synonymous with being a one-person act. As you stand in who you are, you will always need the help and support of others; seek and accept the help when you need it.

- **FIND YOUR INNER PURPOSE.** What were you created to do? What burns inside you to go beyond your roles as mom, wife, business owner, teacher, etc.? If all the titles were taken away, what would be your purpose? Recently, I discovered my purpose, and as I look back, I realize that as I've been living as my authentic self, I've been living out my purpose. The two are firmly connected.

Discover and live life as your authentic self! After all, why would you cover a masterpiece with cheap house paint?

> *For we are God's masterpiece. He has created us anew in Christ Jesus, so we can do the good things he planned for us long ago.* ~ Ephesians 2:10 (NLT)

Now It's Time To Invest

Take time this week to consider who you are — the authentic you. In this time of reflection, consider whether you have cloaked the real you in any area.

If you have been hiding you, answer these two tough questions. Why, and do you want to uncloak?

If uncloaking is your decision, what are your plans to do so?

Build Your Confidence and Live Your Story

I love going to the movies. Give me a great movie, a bucket of theater popcorn, and a comfortable chair, and I am set. Have you ever seen the movie *Big Mama*? Martin Lawrence plays FBI agent Malcolm Turner, who goes undercover as a southern granny named Big Mama to capture a bad guy and protect the beautiful Sherry Pierce and her son. Along the way, Agent Turner, portraying Big Mama, falls for the beautiful girl. I know the typical plot, but watching him attempt to stay in character is funny. There were times that "Big Mama" responded from the heart of Malcolm, making situations awkward and uncomfortable.

For many people, living a double life is part of their daily existence, and the reality is far from funny. Their confidence in themselves is so low that they change with the crowd, like Martin Lawrence in the movie, changing costumes, voices, opinions, habits, likes, and life stories all to stay in character. It's impossible to live your life true to your story if you read from the scripts of other people's lives using their opinions as your opinions, using their looks as a measuring rod for your looks, and determining your success based on their success.

That may be extreme, but do you have an area that you need to build confidence in yourself, an area that you struggle with? It's quite possible to be very confident in one area and lacking in another. Let's take the next few days to build your confidence so you can live your story to the fullest.

If you have an area or if you say, "Nicole, paragraph 2 is me", one of the first things you need to do is axe self-sabotaging habits and behaviors. Two of the biggies in this area are negative self-talk and comparison.

- **NEGATIVE SELF-TALK** — You talk to yourself more than anyone else; it's important to be mindful of what you communicate to yourself. Don't spit discouraging and belittling dialogue! Girl, you better tell yourself you are the boss, you can accomplish the task before you, and you are smart, beautiful, intelligent, and worth your weight in gold! Let you know that you believe in yourself! If no one else in the world believes in you, you can still succeed if you believe in yourself. However, the moment you don't believe in yourself, you have lost the battle.
- **COMPARISON** — Do something for me, compare the mountains of Honduras with the mountains of Japan, and convince me which is the most beautiful and most valuable. Compare Vincent Van Gogh's *The Starry Night* with Leonardo da Vinci's *Mona Lisa*. There is no comparison; you cannot compare two masterpieces. You, my dear lady, are a masterpiece, an original design, inside and out; there is no other like you. Even your

DNA speaks of your individuality. It bothers me as people compare their true selves to the public version of someone else. Hear me now, Queen, there are flaws behind their masks. Do not compare yourself; you are an original. Accept that, embrace that, and with all of your heart, celebrate that!

Next, I want you to make a new friend. Your new friend is yourself. Think of how you make a new friend: you get to know them, spend time together, learn to laugh together, encourage each other, find the good, and forgive one another for shortcomings. Make friends with yourself. Ladies, we are often harder on ourselves than anyone else. We will be there for everyone, forgive for everything, support in every way, compliment in every situation, and encourage at every opportunity. However, when it comes to self, we break out the chopping block, the rule book, and the measuring stick! Give yourself grace. Start being your own new and encouraging friend.

The final will probably be the most challenging: stop seeking approval from others. When I tell you, this sets me free!!! I hear the chains falling right now! Everyone has an opinion, and some get a little unhappy when they can't make their opinion your opinion. I had to come to a point, and you should too, where I refused to allow someone else's opinion to chip at my self-confidence and prevent me from living my story. After all, this is MY story, not yours or ours! I refuse to allow the box that others construct to close me in to keep me from living my life to the fullest. Do you know what happens when someone disapproves of you? NOTHING, unless you allow it to affect your life. It's your choice.

If you want to enjoy the most incredible level of success in your life as a wife, mother, entrepreneur, CEO, writer, politician, or whatever your aspirations include, you must build your confidence so you can live your story loud and proud.

Go ahead, girl, like a boss, be who you are with confidence, and live your story with pride! You got this!

> *One of the lessons that I grew up with was to always stay true to yourself and never let what somebody else says distract you from your goals.* ~ Michelle Obama

Now It's Time To Invest

This week, think of something you can do for yourself by yourself. Take you, your new BFF, out for some quality time. Eileen Caddy said, "It's important from time to time to slow down, to go away by yourself, and simply be." Take that time. Think about who you are, and strengthen your new friendship with encouragement.

After you return from your time away, journal where you went, what you learned, and anything else you want to hold onto to remind you of this day.

Do you hesitate to give your opinion, even when asked, especially around certain people? Why do you hold back your thoughts? You have more than you know to offer.

Teatime — Invest in Your Future

Hellllooooooo everyone! Yes, I must occasionally greet you with my current signature greeting. This week, it really seems to fit as a friendly way to begin my invitation. This week I want to invite you to teatime. Of course, you don't have to drink tea; you choose tea, water, coffee, or soda. The beverage is not important; it's the concept that I want you to grab.

This week, schedule one hour daily in a quiet spot, just you, this journal, a pen, and your beverage of choice. Please note that I did not mention any electronic device. Stop shaking. You will be alright; you can do this. Turn off the volume and leave all devices in another room. When selecting your spot, make sure it's conducive to quiet thinking. Typically, your office, the kitchen, and the bedroom are poor choices; they contain too many visual distractions. Be intentional in your space selection.

Once you settle in, I want you to invest in your future by taking mental time for yourself. This week, schedule daily appointments with yourself and spend time with yourself. Here are a few ideas; use some or choose your own, as this is your time. Just remember the basic rules: sitting alone, quiet, no technology.

- **REFLECT ON YOUR PERSONAL GOALS.** This isn't the time to plan your next boss move or how to fund the college plans for your children; this is personal, all about you. What are your personal goals, and what is your plan to move closer toward them?

- **INVEST IN WHAT'S ESSENTIAL.** When was the last time you invested in yourself personally, not because you needed it but simply because you wanted it? The price is not the issue, so don't let your financial situation talk you out of investing in yourself. It could be taking yourself to lunch, getting a massage, driving two hours to walk on the beach, taking a trip overseas just to see the sights or anything in between. The bottom line is that you must get into the habit of investing in yourself personally. Some of you will not make it through this week's challenge. Guilt will cause you to allow someone or something else to steal this hour from you. Although you will convince yourself, you will make it up. Liar, liar, pants on fire! Your success is connected to your ability to invest in yourself.

- **LOOK AT YOUR VISION BOARD.** WHAT!?! You don't have a vision board? Well, we need to work on that. A vision board is a visible reminder of where you're going. My board gets me excited about the journey when I get bogged down by the details. I was sharing my board with one of my sister friends yesterday, and I got excited again. Excitement is contagious. She is going to create her first board. Yes, I'm shocked, too, someone who has known me for over 25 years, and she doesn't have a board. That has me thinking about where I went wrong with her! But we are correcting that, so it's good. For those with a vision board, take it to one of these sessions and spend some time with it. I promise it will reignite your passion, stir up gratitude, and renew your zeal.

You will never see your dreams and visions become realities unless you invest in them. Investments are not just financial; you must invest your time, and that time investment includes investing in the most important team member — yourself! Even small investments weekly will lead to forward movement. Invest in you; the returns will amaze you!

Invest in yourself to the point it makes someone
else want to invest in you. ~ Tony Gaskins

Now It's Time To Invest

This week, take time to invest in yourself. Use the ideas in this journal or come up with your own. However, do begin by spending time in a quiet spot each day. If you can't afford an hour, invest what you can. This is a guilt-free zone.

Believe in Yourself

*I believe in me. There is no obstacle that I see will be
too hard for me. I know where my help comes from,
and I know that He's got me.* ~ Nikea Marie, Sister

*I wasn't going to let one person's opinion dislodge everything
I thought I knew about myself. Instead, I switched my
method without changing my goal.* ~ Michelle Obama

*"I'm scared of you" live by that. Your confidence
comes from within.* ~ Nikki, Daughter

*Never be limited by other people's limited
imaginations.* ~ Mae Jemison

*No one can make you feel inferior without
your consent.* ~ Eleanor Roosevelt

*When you're on center stage expect cheers and
criticism. Use both to get better.* ~ John Watkis

*We are not the sum total of our weaknesses
and failures.* ~ Pope John Paul II

Talk in the Mirror

I want us to do something different this week. Let's change the scenery. Most of us have a special place to read. This week, I want to ask you to move your comfortable reading spot as we work through *Talk in the Mirror*. It will initially seem strange, but it's ok; the result will be worth a little discomfort.

Go to the mirror that you usually look in. You know, the one you put on makeup or check out your clothes in, yes, that one. Now, look at the person in the mirror. Do you realize that's the person who talks to you more than anyone else? That person has participated in every success and failure in your life. She made all your bad decisions and all your good choices; she picked them.

Often, I hear women talking about what they don't like about themselves: physically, emotionally, educationally, relationally, or financially. I think I've heard it all, and honestly, I have said some of it to myself. Do you know what I discovered that changed my whole world? That chick I see in the mirror every morning is the only one who can change me, and she is the only one who can cause me to accept what is not changeable.

Yep, you're right; it's easier said than done, but change is possible. I have two daughters and two bonus daughters (you may call them daughters-in-law); I own three child development centers and am a coach and pastor. For more than 30 years, I have been surrounded by women, and I'm telling you, if you stick to it, you will see and feel the difference.

Trust me on this one; all I want you to do is ACT NOW. Tell the beautiful and ready-to-change lady in the mirror, "We are going to ACT NOW, baby!" Get a little radical with her, make her laugh, and cause her to hope and believe in herself and the possibility that she has the power to change some things! I have a friend who uses dry-erase markers on her mirror to remind herself to ACT NOW. I surround myself with word art to remind me to ACT NOW. Whatever works for you, let's get ready to ACT NOW.

- **ACCEPT YOURSELF.** Right now, just as you are, you are worthy of love and respect without changing a single thing. You must accept that as the truth. Tell yourself repeatedly. Embrace yourself with all your strengths and weaknesses, wrinkles and flaws. Highlight the positive and stop pointing at what you see as unfavorable. Don't allow yourself to speak critically to you any longer. Talk in the mirror about it.
- **CHANGE THE WAY YOU TREAT YOU.** Terminate the habit of leaving yourself the leftovers of your time, energy, resources, love, and care. Sometimes, you must be first. After all, you are valuable, and your

dreams, goals, and desires are important. Develop habits that keep your mind and body fit and strong. Block time for you like you block time for everyone else; yes, add you to your calendar. Invest in yourself as you invest in others. When you change how you treat yourself, others will change how they treat you.

- **TALK TO YOU LIKE YOU LOVE YOU.** Talk to yourself, verbally and mentally, like you are your best friend and not your worst enemy. I check myself sometimes and ask myself why I said that to myself. I wouldn't talk to others like that, so why would I speak to me like that? Negative thoughts will slip in, push them right back out, and refuse to allow them to slip past your teeth! And while we are on the subject, don't let others talk you down or speak negatively to you about you or your vision. What you will not accept from yourself certainly shouldn't be taken from others.

- **NOTE ADJUSTMENTS YOU NEED TO MAKE.** As you talk to the chick in the mirror, note the adjustments you need to make to create the changes you want to see. Do you need to begin exercising, drink more water, change your circle of associates, or alter what you allow to influence your decisions? It's your list. Word of caution: your plans will fail if you go too deep too fast. If your list of adjustments includes starting today drinking only water and eating only kale for the next six weeks or cutting out television for six weeks when you're a tv-a-holic, you may be setting yourself up to fail. Ensure your adjustments are attainable. Slow and steady beats fast and fail every time; ask the tortoise and the hare.

- **OFFER FORGIVENESS TO YOURSELF.** Let go of the past and move on. Take any decisions you regret and turn them into opportunities to learn.

Make amends where possible and resolve to handle things better in the future. Lose the albatross that others attempt to drape around your neck because they can't forgive you. After you have done all you can, it's their decision to carry the unnecessary burden of unforgiveness, not your responsibility.

- **WORK ON LIKING YOU.** Don't devise a list you allow to sit with the other dusty lists you've created. Really work on liking and loving the person in the mirror. Learn to treat her with kindness and respect. Set goals and see yourself achieving them. Practice, practice, practice, and soon, what you practice will become second nature.

You are with yourself more than anyone else; learn to like who you are, change what you decide to change, and accept what cannot be changed. Embrace the wonderful, unique you. Talk in the mirror and watch her grow! Remember, you are the only one with the power to change the chick in the mirror. Talk to her about it. Be bold, be beautiful, and be you!

Thank you for making me so wonderfully complex! It is amazing to think about. Your workmanship is marvelous— and how well I know it. ~ Psalms 139:14 (TLB)

Now It's Time To Invest

Take each letter in the acrostic ACT NOW and write at least one thing you are willing to do in this area for change.

A – _____

_____

C – _____

_____

T – _____

_____

N – _____

_____

O – _____

_____

W – _____

_____

Make a date with yourself to come back to this page in a month and see how you are doing. Yes, put you on your calendar.

Love Yourself — Be Yourself

Do you have a current favorite picture of yourself? I said current on purpose. For some people, their favorite photo of themselves is years old. We'll talk about that in a moment, but for now, get that current favorite photo of yourself.

Do you have it in hand? Now look that woman in the eye and say the following so she can hear you.

Here I Come!!!!

The woman you see here is confident!
The woman you see here understands her purpose and assignment!
The woman you see here had to go through some things to get here!
The woman you see here is not ashamed of all her failures!
The woman you see here was always here; she just discovered who she IS!!!

Repeat it, and this time, don't *just* read the words; own what you say.

Now my question is, are you ashamed or afraid to be yourself? I'm not the "yourself" you have become to please and appease the world. I'm talking about yourself, your authentic self. In my coaching, conferences, workshops, ministry, and one-on-one interactions, I often speak to women about being their authentic selves. There was a time when I was surprised by some of the women I encountered who walked heavy, looked absolutely gorgeous, reeked with confidence, and seemed to have success by the tail, only to learn they were holding back their authentic selves. They had a hidden storage box filled with shame, fear, and battered confidence that hindered them from earnestly loving and being their genuine self.

It is impossible to love who you are and be who you are if you are not who you truly are. If you are the sum total of who your parents said, who your husband wants, who your children need, who the business world values, who your church members accept, and who society celebrates, then where is there space for you to be yourself?

What does it mean to be your authentic self? Your authentic self is who you are deep down. The part of you that doesn't care what others think. Authenticity happens when your words, actions, and behaviors consistently match your core identity. Some, who have become so accustomed to the version everyone loves and are slaying what they do with success, would ask, "Why is that important? I'm doing good." I say good is not good enough. There is greatness in you that is being concealed by the good. If you had five million dollars in the bank, would you be satisfied with only having access to 50 thousand dollars? Wealth and riches are right there, and they belong to you, yet your access is reduced to limited wealth. No, that's not acceptable. Another side of being your authentic self is summed up in a quote that I love: "The sooner you are authentically you, the sooner the people looking for you will find you." I don't know who initially said that, but they were on point. Finally, you will never know the extreme joy of being and loving yourself until you discover and allow yourself to become the real YOU.

Learning to be your authentic self is essential to building meaningful relationships. Years ago, a young lady got married and, within a week, dedicated her life to Christ. There was so much shame and damaged self-esteem from the life she had lived that she started allowing changes to occur in the way she thought, how she responded, and even how she dressed. She became what she assumed a good wife and Christian should be. Nine years later, sitting in her car in front of Burlington Coat Factory, her proverbial light came on, and she realized she lost who she was somewhere in trying to be what she thought she should be. At first, her husband was shocked; he had to get to know his wife as she was getting reacquainted with herself. They have been together for more than 30 years at this point, and he would tell you the version of herself she was for the first nine years would not have weathered the storms they have stood against. His successes and the fire of their relationship have been empowered by his wife being her authentic self. People may like the knock-off version of the Louis Vuitton handbag, but it could never compare to the genuine and original version.

Someone recently asked me two questions on this subject, "Were you ever afraid to be your authentic self? Do you have to square your shoulders and lift your head more purposefully when you enter unfamiliar territory with new people, especially people who, by the world's standards, have arrived at a place you are striving to reach?" I answered, "I don't think I've ever been afraid to be my authentic self. I wanted people to know I am not perfect. I have a few insecurities, but they don't have me bound."

As I pen this journal, I am about to walk into a room I have never entered, but I feel I belong. I can add value by sharing my experiences as well. My Dad always made me feel I could do anything. He encouraged my boldness when I was a young teenager. I was ok with being different, and my peers respected me for the difference. I was never embarrassed to tell people I was a virgin. I still was that cool kid in school, liked by guys but very much respected. So, as an adult, business owner, and entrepreneur without a 4-year college degree in a field where the "sheepskin" is a door opener, I had to stand in my truth. I had to let people know I was living my dream without regret. I enjoy being who I am, and I love myself.

Earlier, I specifically asked you to get a current photo. Love who you are today. Yes, years bring physical changes. Embrace the beautiful you now; don't get lost in what you looked like years ago. No one can do you but you. No one can be the best version of you but you. Love yourself — flaws and all — and be yourself out loud and on purpose. You are amazing!

Today, you are you! That is truer than true! There
is no one alive who is you-er than you! Shout loud
'I am lucky to be what I am.' ~ Dr. Seuss

Now It's Time To Invest

Schedule a photoshoot! It can be a family member or a friend taking pictures of you with their phone. Dress cute, cute... like fire cute! Go someplace out of your norm: a park, stream, favorite store in the mall, construction site, whatever works for you. Now enjoy taking photos of your beautiful and fantastic self — your right now self!

Want to be adventurous? Print your favorite 2 or 3 photos from your shoot. Display them in your world, home, work, and social media.

Journal about your journey to be yourself and love yourself.

Putting Yourself in Timeout

Have you ever wanted to stand in the middle of the floor, on top of a table, or in aisle 6 of a grocery store and scream to the top of your lungs? With your fists defiantly clenched, yelling, "I'M PUTTING MYSELF IN TIME OUT!" No? Oh, maybe it's just me! Imagine how everyone would look at you like you have just totally lost control except, of course, the others who would join you. Maybe we should try it? No? Ok then, let's be safe and just talk about it.

Most of us have a packed schedule; I know I do. However, in the busyness, I have discovered the value of rest, sometimes the hard way. Notice I didn't say sleep; that is also valuable, but let's talk rest for now. Rest is a state of decreased bodily work, physical and or mental, designed to leave you renewed, refreshed, and rejuvenated. Rest includes the whole being.

Do you know that God rested? He commanded rest for the land and people. Before scientists discovered the power of rest, God already knew. Rest supports mental health, increases creativity, concentration, and memory, reduces stress, improves health, and puts you in a better mood.

I've heard people apologize for needing to rest! As vital as it is, do you feel guilty about taking that time out? As you seek to live a more balanced life, you must consider relaxation times a crucial part of your schedule.

There are many ways to rest and relax; it's your assignment to discover what works for you. Here are some ideas. To give your mind a 10-15 minute rest during the day, try pushing away from screen time: phones, computers, television, and such. You can also sit quietly or with soft music in the background while focusing on nothing or try zoning out while mindlessly watching birds fly or cars pass. All of these offer an opportunity for your mind to disengage briefly, similar to restarting a computer.

For extended periods of relaxation, consider a long bath or short walk, feed the ducks, date yourself to a movie, spa, or lunch, or curl up on the couch with a good novel. Notice I did not say a book about your business, children, or ministry; remember, you are in a time-out.

This is your time to rest and relax; you decide what works best for you based on time, desire, and likes. It is essential to see the value of relaxation and to protect the time you schedule to rest. Before you start, let your family and others know you are in a time-out. Otherwise, they will assume you are available since you "seem" free and innocently impose on your time.

Listen to your body; it will give clues about when to rest. Have you ever "lost a thought" and had to go back to find it? CLUE. In the middle of a conversation, have you stopped mid-sentence because your mind went blank for a few seconds? CLUE. If you ever do the screaming exercise mentioned in the first paragraph — BIG CLUE. Listen to your body and enjoy the rest.

Sometimes the most productive thing you
can do is rest. ~ Mark Black

Now It's Time To Invest

What are some of the ways you use or think you would like to use to rest?
Write down a few ideas for quick rests and longer times of relaxation.

This week, try some of the ideas you wrote down and journal your outcome.

If it applies, how did your family respond to your rest and relaxation announcement? Remember, as you are learning, so are they.

How to Tell Your Story

In October 2022, at my first mansion retreat, I was super excited to have Mr. John Watkis as a key speaker. I had the privilege of attending one of his sessions at another retreat in January of the same year. He is a multi-talented man, but this day, his assignment was to teach us how to tell our story.

Regardless of your occupation, there will be times you will be asked to share your "story." This request leaves people with questions: "What does that mean? What is the purpose? How do I narrow my life into a 5-minute speech? Who wants to hear about my life?" and more. The unanswered questions often leave people a little uneasy and uncertain.

Mr. Watkis took his time to walk us through the power of the story within each of us. I take no credit for the notes written here. I attended the session just as the other retreat attendees, and just like the others, I walked away with a new vision of the story of Nicole L. Brown. I walked away motivated and encouraged with a sense of power as I understood the potential of my story lived and told.

I will share a snippet of what he gave us that morning. However, if you ever have the opportunity to sit in one of his sessions, don't sleep on it; sit in the front row.

The power of your story is that it allows you to connect with others. Connecting to others is essential in business, ministry, or at the corner store. As an entrepreneur, leader, or parent, the ability to connect with others through your story will cause them to see themselves in what you've done, connecting both of you to what they are experiencing. Even sharing your story in simple conversations with others, such as sales conversations, will cause strangers to connect with you. If you are a Christian, they will be presented with the opportunity to connect to Christ. In all instances, connection occurs if the story is told well.

Your story tells why you do what you do. As it is your original story, there's no other like it; therefore, its presentation must be authentic. The genuine presentation is filled with truth, sounds, feelings, smells, fears, joys, successes, and failures that come together to tell the true story of you. Most will never be asked to share their entire life story in one setting; therefore, it's important to determine by the situation, audience, and event what portion of your story you are to present.

Some elements should be present in every story: time, place, what life was like, who the characters were, what the challenge was, how you responded, how you felt, what you did do, what was the end result, and the lesson learned.

- **SCENE SET.** This helps to create the picture by setting the scene. People need to know where and when this portion of your story occurs. For example, you can creatively share the "when" by establishing the date or grade you were in. The location could be in the woods or in Germany. It gives the listener information to form the scene. For example, *One summer night on a balcony overlooking the streets of Paris...*

- **GLIMPSE OF LIFE.** What was life like, and who were the people and relationships of this portion of your story? You must give the listener what they need to paint the scene; this step puts people and action into play. For example, *my husband and I sat beside each other, gazing quietly over the city.*

- **REVEAL THE CHALLENGE.** Every story needs a challenge, a moment where a decision is required; otherwise, what's the story's point? For example, *As we sat in silence, I struggled in my mind to grasp the fullness of God's goodness in our lives. When I considered where we began and where God had brought us, the many ways He had blessed our family, my heart filled with gratitude that I could not express.*

- **RESPONSE AND FEELINGS.** The authenticity of your story is intertwined with what happens inside of you. For a genuine connection, people need to know the internal narrative and how you felt and responded. Yes, even when the feelings are not positive and even when the actions are unfavorable. Transparency and connection require honesty in the good and the bad. For example, *I was so full that I wanted to cry, sing, and worship all at once. I wanted to yell to the people on the streets of Paris about my amazing God and His faithfulness. Instead, I did the most remarkable thing I could have done.*

- **WHAT DID YOU DO?** This is where you share what you ultimately decided to do, even if your decision was wrong. It's ok to share the mistakes; people need to see that there are no perfect people, so there are no perfect stories. Share your decision. For example, *I gently reached for Steve's hand as we continued for a moment to sit in the quiet worship and adoration of our God and the life He gave us.*

- **WHAT WERE THE RESULTS, AND WHAT LESSONS DID YOU LEARN?** Your story will be incomplete unless you share what happened when you did what you did and what lessons you learned. In every story, point to the lessons learned because I assure you every situation has a message if you are willing to learn. For example, At that moment, I fell in love a little deeper with my husband and my God. I learned the power of quiet inner worship born from gratitude and the closeness of a man after God's own heart.

When I adhere to the example, my quick story becomes this:

One summer night, on a balcony overlooking the streets of Paris, my husband and I sat beside each other, gazing quietly over the city. As we sat in silence, I struggled in my mind to grasp the fullness of God's goodness in our lives. When I considered where we began, where God had brought us, and the many ways He had blessed our family, my heart filled with gratitude that I could not express. I was so full that I wanted to cry, sing, and worship all at once. I wanted to yell to the people on the streets of Paris about my amazing God and His faithfulness. Instead, I did the most remarkable thing I could have done. I gently reached for Steve's hand as we continued for a moment to sit in the quiet worship and adoration of our God and the life He gave us. At that moment, I fell in love a little deeper with my husband and my God. I learned the power of quiet inner worship born from gratitude and the closeness of a man after God's own heart.

Here are some random golden nuggets from that day.

- When you share your story, trust your preparation's power and ability. Fear may come but share it anyway.
- The ability to communicate is essential. People will form an opinion of where you belong based on how you speak. Your voice is the calling card they will remember.
- *"Comparison is the thief of joy."*
- You aren't the hero of every story; we all make mistakes. In telling your story, be vulnerable and willing to share the good, bad, and ugly.

With every door that opens for you to share your story, remember to stand confident in your delivery and never compare yourself to another. Someone needs to hear your story. It doesn't have to be a perfect story perfectly told; your part is to share. You got this! Yes, you can do this!"

> *I have better stories from the mistakes I've made than I do from my successes. Even though I may not have handled it right at the moment, I have the lessons I learned to pass on.* ~ John Watkis

Now It's Time To Invest

What is one portion of your life that you seem to share the most? Take that portion and revamp how you tell your story using the notes here. Share it with someone you trust once you have it fresh and revised. What were the differences between how you used to share and the revamped version?

Balancing Who You Are

Have you heard the caution not to become a public success and a private failure? I have, too. The sad part is that some of the people I've heard sharing the warning have later had their private lives exposed, revealing their gross contradicting failures behind the curtain.

Anyone who knows me knows I am about the hustle and grind! I'm not seeking success in one lane; I'm in several and working at growth in all simultaneously. I put in the work required to succeed and carry as many with me as possible! I share victories openly on various social media platforms, not to brag, but because it's part of the marketing plan connected to my life as an entrepreneur coach. In all that, with all that, in this one thing, I am determined; I will not allow my private life to fall apart to be successful in public. When I say my private life, I mean my relationship with God, my family, myself, and my close circle.

Many ask me, "Nicole, how do you do it? Girl, it seems you are everywhere doing everything. How do you keep it all together?" My answer simply stated is balancing who you are. However, the mechanics of the balancing act can get complicated. For all I'm doing, my family is doing just as much. Steve, my husband, is a senior pastor of a thriving, community-impacting ministry and the owner of a financial and tax service company. My children are a success story in the making: my son is a professional basketball player overseas, my godson is a college basketball coach, and my daughters are entrepreneurs with thriving and demanding businesses. I support and remain connected to all of that. Between what they do, what I do, and everything else around, it seems like it could be an overload and only allow enough time, energy, and resources for the bare minimum of support. But the "bare minimum" in everything will never lead to great success in anything. I had to come up with a system.

My system of balancing who I am has three essential components at its core.

1. **CHECKPOINTS** — I am constantly checking in, communicating, and listening to God, my immediate family, and my close circle. This core group lets me know if I am out of balance and need to shift. I remain sensitive to the words spoken, the words not spoken, and the visual clues. Through my relationships and interactions, I am reminded of what is vital versus what is important. I listen, see, and respond. I can't overstress the value of checkpoints. I believe many fail in this area because the right people do not have their ears. They begin to listen to the voices of the hustle and grind. They give value to the voices of others who are clawing their way to the top at the expense of what is most important. They attempt to momentarily shift their focus, intent

on turning it back after a season. However, the seasons continue to change, and the world behind the curtain crumbles around them in what seems like a blink of an eye. My relationship with God, my family, and my close circle are vital in my ability to balance who I am.

2. **SUPPORT TEAM** — There is no way I could accomplish what I do without my incredible support team that does what they do. I have gifted and talented people surrounding me who carry out what is necessary for my businesses to flourish daily. They do the things I do not have to do. I determine what I must do in every business assignment and what can be delegated to a team member. Honestly, this was a big challenge for me as a young entrepreneur. As the owner and CEO, I thought I had to have my finger on everything. That thinking limited my success and growth capacity and stretched me thin. If you have 1 or 100 people on your support team, communicate your vision, train them, empower them with responsibility and authority, and see how they will surprise you. Word of caution: don't be surprised if you select a few that don't last. You are learning how to choose, and people are learning where they fit. Don't allow the frustration of a few choices that didn't work to send you back to doing it all yourself. It's all part of balancing who you are.

3. **UNITY** — Who I am is contained in one body. I could not physically separate Nicole, the entrepreneur, from Nicole, the wife; she is the same person held in the same body. On the same note, I find that to balance who I am, I cannot separate my world. My family knows my close circle, and they intertwine. My close circle has the access code to my home, and they know where to find the paper towels. The members

of my support teams know my family and my close circle. Within this group, we celebrate the wins, pray through the challenges, cry through the losses, and rally to support each other at some level, no matter what. I don't have a sense of being torn within my world, and each supports the other. When my family and I travel overseas to spend holidays with my son and his wife (my bonus daughter), all hands are on deck to ensure everything is taken care of in my absence. Once I had significant health challenges, members of my close circles gathered to work with my business support team to ensure the essential requirements were completed. I have one world, and it operates in unity.

Balancing who you are isn't something you accomplish and forget. You must continue to work to maintain, but it's worth your efforts. You can do this!

After defining success in a way that includes
your loved ones, the next step is to adjust your
priorities to reflect that. ~ John Maxwell

Now It's Time To Invest

Do you struggle to balance the various roles and assignments in your life? Write down some ways you attempt to balance who you are between these roles and assignments.

Analyze what you wrote above. Are these working? For the ones that are supporting your efforts, keep it going. For the attempts you are making that are not working, can you tweak them for better use, or do you need to eliminate them?

Who is on your support team? Have you communicated your vision, trained, and empowered them with responsibility and authority? If your support team is constantly asking you, "What's next?" reevaluate you and the team. Brainstorm your thoughts here.

Love Yourself

*Be proud of who you are and not ashamed of
how someone else sees you.* ~ Unknown

*I praise you because of the wonderful way you
created me. Everything you do is marvelous! Of
this I have no doubt.* ~ Psalm 139:14 (CVE)

*You are allowed to be both a masterpiece and a work
in progress simultaneously.* ~ Sophia Bush

Talk to yourself like someone you love. ~ Brene Brown

Seek to be whole, not perfect. ~ Oprah

*You alone are enough, you have nothing to
prove to anybody.* ~ Dr. Maya Angelou

*If you have the ability to love, love yourself
first.* ~ Charles Bukowski

*Don't forget to say I love you to the dearest person
in the world, YOURSELF.* ~ Unknown

Family

We Kissed Under the Most Romantic Bridge in Paris

I have this close circle of sister-friends, and we have been together since before my oldest child was born. We've acquired the name *The Original Golden Girls*. Don't ask me how or why; it just works for us. Many years ago, we were at a restaurant discussing our marriages; we are each other's safe place. At some point, we realized that we could not be married to any spouse in the group except our own. We concluded that we were the best pick for them and vice versa. We laughed; that's something we do a lot and continued to eat; that's something else we do a lot.

I share that to emphasize that this week is not intended to be a road map of *15 Tips to Return Fire to Your Marriage* or *10 Sure Proof Ways to Make Your Lover Happy*. Your marriage is just as unique as you and your husband. The specifics of what Steve and I do in our marriage to build unity and intimacy may not render the same results in your marriage. Knowing your marriage and discovering what works for you and your man is essential.

I love my husband, and I really like him. I can honestly say he is my best friend, but that wasn't always the case. We enjoy a great marriage. Together, we have worked to get to this point and continue to invest in our relationship because we know there is more. We also continue to work because we still encounter days, situations, and mindsets within each other that lead to, we'll say, "heated fellowship."

The following golden tidbits are not the total of what we do, just some I thought valuable to share.

- We are committed to God, each other, our marriage, and our family. That word commitment to us has an old-school definition and bond, not a new-age loophole. It's a loyalty encased in responsibility and woven into our every decision and action.
- We believe in each other — our character, dreams, heart, and intent. Our trust in one another is locked in tight. Our belief in each other causes us to invest in each other. We invest time, money, heart, understanding, and talents; we pour everything we have into each other. No one, absolutely no one, supports Steve and his dreams more than I do. The most significant investor in my dreams and endeavors is, guess who, you got it, Steve.
- We make our marriage a priority. We both have busy lives, but we are the priority, and we make that known to each other and the people in our lives.
- We manage the rough spots. Letting an issue go unresolved or sweeping a difference under the rug is dangerous. As a couple, you will never

settle what you attempt to hide. It's not always easy to communicate about challenges, and sometimes it seems easier to shut down. However, shutting down erects a quiet and deadly wall of division.

- We spend time together. We don't limit our time together to a specific portion of the day or night, a set idea or place, or a particular activity. The spontaneity adds to the excitement. Steve coming out of his office and saying, "You wanna grab something to eat" at midday always makes me smile. It says he has a break and wants me a part of that time. I and we, as a couple, are valuable to him. We plan quick getaways and trips. Ok, truth, I usually do the planning, and there was a time that bothered me. I wanted him to plan and surprise me sometimes. Then I matured; this is one of my strengths, one of the things I bring to our marriage, and I am great at it. I can turn a weekend into a fantasy dream come true, and what I can do with a layover in another country would make you drool with envy! Just as I use my strengths to build and invest in our marriage, so Steve uses his; as I said, I learned this when I matured.

- We protect each other and our privacy. There are certain things we would never discuss with others. However, when we need to talk to someone else concerning our marriage, we only use our safe places. Our safe places are very few, and they are people who love us both. People who have no problem saying, "Nicole, you are wrong. You need to fix that and start with I'm sorry." People who know us well enough to get the whole story and not just the version we present. People who would never look at either of us differently because they love us both. And people who pray for us.

Have you wondered why I selected the title *"We Kissed Under the Most Romantic Bridge in Paris?"* It actually happened, and looking back, it was a mark in time that reminds me of my husband and our amazing life together. What would you title your journal about your marriage? Let me encourage you, regardless of the state of your marriage, to invest in improving it. If you are single and plan to marry one day, continue to work on yourself while gathering information to prepare you for marriage.

> *This explains why a man leaves his father and*
> *mother and is joined to his wife, and the two*
> *are united into one.* ~ Genesis 2:24 (NLT)

Now It's Time To Invest

How do you define commitment?

If you are married, how do you and your husband show commitment? If you're single and desire to be married one day, what are ways that you desire your husband to show his commitment to you and your marriage?

What is one thing you can do today to make your husband smile? Do it. If you are single and want to be married one day, what could your husband do to make you smile?

Let Them Know

I enjoy walking into my kitchen and having my breath taken away by a gorgeous bouquet from Steve. Not a holiday, birthday, or makeup bouquet, just a beautiful vase of flowers. Likewise, Steve appreciates it when I go shopping and return with something he likes. I can tell by the way he says, "Thanks, babe," while looking at the newest addition to his world. In both instances, we are saying one to another, "I was thinking about you today. I love you."

When I was younger, I wasn't a big flower fan; maybe I never put much effort into their meaning. However, with age comes wisdom. Now, I absolutely love it when others let me know I was on their mind and that they love me. Remember the last time someone special surprised you with a gesture of love and appreciation? Recall how amazing that made you feel. What an incredible feeling! No matter what kind of day you are having, everything suddenly changes.

When was the last time you stopped to let the people in your life know that you think of them and love them? Children, parents, spouses, friends, cousins, grandparents, staff, business partners, and others in your world need to know they are important to you.

People say, "Tomorrow isn't promised to anyone." Then they live life like they have the promise of forever. They put off making that call, taking that trip, sending that card, and investing that time with the promise of tomorrow. And then one day, tomorrow is not possible. I thank God that, as much as possible, I've invested in the people I love. As much as I miss my Mom, Papa (my grandfather), brother, aunt, father-in-law, and other very special people we have had to say so long to, I know they knew I loved and valued them. I'm grateful that when my children were young, I let them know how much I love and cherish them with my words and deeds. I made the calls, invested the time, and made the drives, showing and telling them their great value in my life.

Tell them how much you love them and their importance to your world. Who in your world needs to hear or see how much you value them? Don't wait for tomorrow; let them know today.

If I had a single flower for every time I think of you, I could walk forever in my garden. ~ Claudia Adrienne Grandi

Now It's Time To Invest

Write down how it makes you feel when someone you love expresses their love and care for you.

Pick 3-5 people this week to show how important they are to you and how much you appreciate them. Select people from various areas of your world. Record your notes here.

Digital Detox

Hey. HEY. HEY! Yep, you. I know you want to run past this section and look for another, but before you do, I ask you to do one thing for yourself and your family. Get your smartphone; most of you will not have to get up because it's beside you. Go to your settings and locate the area that details USAGE. Spend some time right there. Look at daily and weekly usage information. Your phone records how many times you pick it up and which APP you use first after the pickup, how many times you open an APP, what percentage of your time you are on an APP, how many hours a day you are on your phone, and what you are doing. The information it records is crazy and, at times, startling.

While information and research vary, the average person spends 6 hours and 58 minutes on their smartphone, checking approximately 96 times daily, which is about once every 10 minutes. Now, on average, guess how much time families spend together? Ready? 37 minutes a day. If you want to skip this section, go ahead.

For those still with me in this section, I say it's time for us to become very purposeful in disconnecting from our phones to allow us greater opportunities to reconnect or connect more to ourselves, our family, and our friends. Ladies, it's time to get serious about *Digital Detox*.

I've taken steps to clear my life of some of my screen time, but after seeing the statistics I shared and my own USAGE report, well, let me say this coach must go back to training camp! Balance is vital; seven of my waking hours with this little device in my hand is not a good balance. Let's look at some points to help us make the changes we need for ourselves, our families, and our entrepreneurial endeavors.

- I realize my phone sounds like a day in a music box shop; something is constantly ringing, dinging, blinking, or singing. I receive notifications of all calls, texts, social media interactions from all platforms, emails from several accounts, appointments, product releases, shipping updates, doors opening at my house or one of my business locations, and so on. Now, as an entrepreneur, some of that is necessary. However, let's take the time to weed out what is unnecessary for immediate notification, but a scheduled check will suffice. Let's turn off some of those distractions.
- Are social media platforms an integral part of your business? They are for me, and therefore, they require my time and effort. I have people helping me with my social media presence, but I'm still personally very involved. However, I realize I don't have to comment on every happy face and heart. I don't have to track down the lives of those who put in

those negative comments. I don't have to allow social media to lead me on a squirrel chase where one note leads to 15 additional searches, and before I know it, I've invested two hours into nothing worth real value.

- I want to be in that moment when I'm with my family and friends or in a purposed moment alone. While I do a decent job of not allowing the phone to pull me from that time, I know I can do better. For example, I'm the queen of look now, respond later, but could I practice more don't look times? I need to give that some attention, what about you?
- Don't allow what others do or how they live in public to consume you. Enjoy your life. Stay in your world, and don't get lost in others. Don't compare what you have with what you think someone else has. I think I get an A+ in this; however, I still need to stay on guard.
- Be present without your phone. Ok, this one stings; I need to work on this.

Your smartphone should not be more intelligent than you, nor should it have the power to control you and the time you spend with family, friends, or yourself. Time is the one thing we cannot take back. Let's make daily decisions to invest wisely.

"If our phone is always in our presence, it takes away our ability to be present" ~ Author Unknown

Now It's Time To Invest

As you looked through your usage, what did you discover? Where do you require change?

How long can you turn off your phone? Test yourself.

If you and your family or friends are connected to your phones, schedule a no-phone date. Make memories and record them in your mind, not on social media. Record the outcome here — the good, the funny, and the challenging aspects.

There's Nothing Like Family

I still carry and live by many lessons I learned growing up. The most important message taught and lived before me was *There's Nothing Like Family.*

My early memories are filled with family and the power of our unity. My grandfather, Papa, was the leader of the movement to obtain and maintain unity within our family. Papa was the patriarch of the family, and everyone knew it. He was a big man with a big heart who loved his family to the depths of his soul. And although he was a gentle giant, everyone listened to Papa when he spoke.

He purchased an RV, and we would pack in that thing on our way to see the country. The hours on the road taught us to shut out the world and focus on the most vital part of living — family. Laughter was thick as the cousins were on top of cousins, uncles, aunts, mamas, and daddies; we were all present, with Papa and Gigi leading the tribe.

The children in the back of that wonderland on wheels have grown up, and now we have our own children; even though many we love are not physically with us, we continue to keep family first. It's what we were taught; there's nothing like family. I see the influence of those lessons in my life in the man I married. I'm sure his devotion to family is no accident. Together, in little and big ways, we keep family first.

We live in the Washington, DC area, and life has always been busy. As youth pastors and now pastoring a ministry, we have always had revolving doors to our house that is the hub of activity. However, God has always given us the grace to keep family first while giving and investing in others, ministry, businesses, and personal growth. No matter how many other activities attempt to demand priority, we keep family first.

Strong family unity fosters security, internal strength, and the sense that you are never alone. One call, and we rally for the cause. No one is more important than the other; we celebrate the wins, supply the needs, mourn the losses, and intertwined through all that we do, we love each other without condition. There is nothing like family!

My children are adults, and Steve and I are learning how to be the best parents we can be at this stage of their lives. I read once, "Having days together with your grown children is like visiting with the most treasured and beautiful part of your life." That pretty much sums it up! They are the physical proof that investment in your family reaps tremendous rewards.

Let me not paint the picture like everything was perfect! Not so, not so, so not so! But good or bad, there is still nothing like family! And I have found the best time to celebrate them is now.

The happiest moments of my life have been the few which I have passed at home in the bosom of my family. ~ Unknown

Now It's Time To Invest

When was the last time you reached out to a member of your family to share a special memory or to say I love you? This week, select five members of your family and reach out. Now, you can pick the easy ones, or you can really take a significant unity step and reach out to some of the more challenging family members.

What is your funniest memory as a child?

Who made the most significant positive impact on your family? Are you living what they taught you in your family?

Work Life Balance

I read an article that included a survey where participants rated how effectively they balance their work and family life. The options were: (1) happy as can be, (2) I'm on the right track, but I need more time to exercise, (3) not the best I could use a day off, and (4) terrible, I don't know what my family looks like anymore. Only 15% of the participants said they were happy as can be. Notice the option didn't say I'm doing perfectly; I could have understood the low percentage if that were the case. The survey supported what I already know; many are struggling in this vital area, and there is a need for greater efforts in learning creative ways to balance work and home life.

In truth, balancing family and work will always require intentional attention, outside-of-the-box thinking, family communication, and creativity to maintain. I want to share a few tools that have worked for my family and me through the years. However, let me say we have not always maintained the balance. There have been times when we have allowed ourselves to get so far out of balance that we had to forgive each other and pull together to recapture our sense of stability. Every member of the Brown household has always been involved in multiple endeavors. At times, due to our crazy schedules, it would

67

have been easier to allow the disconnectedness to become the norm for our family; however, the value we place on family and our relationships is more important than outside ventures. There is simply nothing like family.

We have found balance at its best when we:

- **PLAN.** We plan for everything else, so why not plan for family time? Be sensible in your planning; if you overpack your calendar with work assignments, appointments, and meetings, anything family you put on the calendar can be squeezed out. In your planning, be creative. I used to take my girls to IHOP for pancakes before school, go to school, have lunch with one of them, sit up and talk to my son after a game, and steal away for an afternoon movie or bike ride with my husband. As we continued to keep our family a priority collectively, we looked for ways to balance our lives.
- **REMAIN FLEXIBLE.** Many don't like change, but sometimes it's required. It's ok to rearrange when necessary. There are certain times of the year we know that based on our assignment, one of us will be busier than the others, and we work together. When we take family vacations, there are times when one of us will arrive later than the others; we work together. Together, we remain flexible. There are times at work you will have to be all right with someone else completing the project; you must stay flexible.
- **COMMUNICATE.** At one time, this was a struggle for the Brown Family, but we kept at it and now benefit from the years of training. In the planning process, plan to let your family know when there will be a season of extra busyness at work. To compensate for the time apart,

spend extra time together upfront or plan for something together at the end of the work crunch. It's also essential to communicate with your boss and let them know a busy time is approaching in your family that will require more of your time and energy. Communication is key.

- **AVOID WASTING TIME.** One of the most useless investments of your time is worry. Worry is sneaky, and it will slip in when least expected. While working on a project, your mind drifts; before you know it, you have tossed 30 minutes down the dark hole of worry. Think about it: that is 30 minutes you could have used to be productive elsewhere. One of the best ways I've found to keep my mind from going idle and entering the worry trap I learned from my husband. He works with numbers and has learned the value of taking breaks to keep his mind sharp and focused. A short walk with the dog, a lunch break, a stretch with a soda break. He is committed to taking breaks, knowing he will be better when he returns, which helps him guard his time.

To balance your work and family life, don't forget to include time for yourself. During our attempts to balance time, especially when you're busy at work or with family, it's easy to forget yourself. Take time for yourself. If you burn out, no one will benefit.

It is possible to balance your family and work life, and while it may be challenging at times, it is always worth it.

The main thing is to keep the main thing
the main thing. ~ Joyce Meyer

Now It's Time To Invest

Specifically, what do you need to do to balance your work and family life better? Are you willing to make the change? How will you approach the change?

This week, log how much time you spend with your family. How did you do?

What creative ways could you use to help you spend more time with your family?

Things My People Say

*Control what you can control (It's a statement
that lets me know I can't control what happens
in every situation, but I can control how I react
and handle it.)* ~ Ricky Feurtado, Godson

*Discipline = legacy. Your ability or inability to
discipline yourself will not only impact you but
generations to come.* ~ Eve Ferguson, Cousin

*If My people who are called by My name will humble
themselves, and pray and seek My face, and turn from
their wicked ways, then I will hear from heaven, and will
forgive their sin and heal their land. 2 Chronicles 7:14*
~ Favorite Scripture of Linda Satterthwaite, Aunt

*Jesus never said that it would feel good, look good,
or even be good, but He promised that it will work
out for the good.* ~ Jada Jackson, Friend

*Don't let your past fear rob you of an opportunity that will
give you an exponential reward — spiritually, mentally,
physically, or monetarily.* ~ Carol Jones, Friend

Keep it moving. ~ (This means do not allow your past or fears to hold you back from moving forward into what God has for you.) Cameron Satterthwaite, Cousin

Let them eat cake. ~ (This is something my Dad always said. People always seem happy when they eat cake, so the idea is to let people be happy.) Donny Ferguson, Cousin

To God be the glory. ~ (This was always my mother's saying if the times were good or bad. It was more than her saying; it was the way she lived her life.) Pam Hooker, Mother

You big dummy. ~ (Papa said this to everyone when they "messed up." Then he would say, "But I love you," and gather the family to help where you needed it. There was so much affection and love wrapped up in those three little words. You felt slighted if he didn't say them to you.) Papa, Grandfather

Feed your family first. ~ Trina Ferguson, Cousin

The things I have created in my life may not be the best, but they are better than the awesome things that others have never put out into the world. ~ TJ Ferguson, Cousin

We're going to have a little family
prayer. ~ Papa, Grandfather

GiGi, my Grandmother's greatest quote is "I love you." Even when she doesn't say it with her words, her actions always say, "I love you." From grilled cheese-making contests to games of *I Declare War* and evenings of dancing like she was the youngest one in the group, GiGi always says, "I love you."

It was not what my Dad, Frank Hooker, said; it's how he says it. One thing everyone who knows him knows is that in the middle of a conversation, he will start a prayer. When you hear him start, that's your cue to join in. When the prayer is over, the conversation continues from where it left off. It's just the way it goes in my family.

Passion

What Season Are You In?

Have you ever seen someone wear clothing in the winter that clearly should be saved for summer? Snow up to the kneecaps, and they have on boots and shorts. They stand out in a crowd because they are dressed out of season. Brrr...they make me shiver as I watch them pass.

A season is a period of time that is identifiable by a certain set of circumstances or conditions. The most obvious example is the seasons of the year. I've learned a few things about seasons that have helped me in my endeavors. First, seasons do not always come as scheduled on the calendar. Have you ever seen a cold front come through during sandal season? It leaves you scurrying for closed-toe shoes and a jacket, right? Second, seasons demand behavior changes. Farmers know well that there is a season to plant and a season to sow; keeping that in mind is beneficial to their crop success. Third, seasons revolve; they do not stand still.

Your dreams, visions, and passionate pursuits are no different; they also have seasons. What's interesting about the seasons of a dream is that they look different for each venture and person. The ability to identify the season you are in as you are in the process of breathing life into your dream is vital. So I ask you, *what season are you in?*

Let's look at a few seasons. Remember, I stated earlier that they revolve and come in no particular order. Just like a cold front can come unexpectedly in the autumn, so can one of these seasons pop up suddenly and unannounced.

- **DREAM.** The dreaming season of your vision should be a continual part of your process; from start to finish and beyond, dreaming is powerful and vital. Dreaming fans the flames of passion like no other. As well, it's in the dreaming that unimaginable plans surface. This season begins the writing time, recording everything even if it makes no sense. I've learned not to challenge my dreams but instead to enjoy them. However, do not stay in the seasons of dreams; your plans will never happen if you only dream.
- **PLAN.** The planning season begins when you write your dreams. It starts as a big picture, advances to a step-by-step goal action plan, and then divides into achievable steps. It's a living thing that continues to grow and develop as you move forward. How important is this season? In the words of one of my mentors, John Maxwell, *"... growth doesn't happen by accident. It's not an automatic process. If you want to guarantee growth, then you need a plan—something strategic, specific, and scheduled."*
- **ACT.** There is a season that demands action; you must move. Take the plan off the paper and let it live. When is that season? Only you will know. I will tell you this: you will never be 100% sure with the writing

on the wall. Usually, I can't explain it; I just know now is the time to act. It's kind of like jumping double dutch; you sway back and forth with the rhythm of the ropes, listening as they slap the ground, and suddenly, you jump. Watching brilliant people with amazing dreams grow dusty, swaying beside the ropes, never jumping in disturbs me.

- **RE-EVALUATE.** Conditions are always prime to re-evaluate. Even if something is going good, is good good enough? Can it be better? We are living in a world of rapid growth in technology. Your plans that began two years ago need a booster shot. Are the employees you hired in the position last year working in an area that maximizes their talents? Is your marketing plan aligned with the resources available today? Re-evaluation keeps your plans relevant to what is happening right now.

- **LEARN.** Learning is always in season. I actively pursue learning — online, in workshops, taking courses, listening to others, reading, forever learning, and applying what I learn to my actions. If you are a learner, you can pick out someone who believes they have learned all there is to know. They become the ultimate expert in their mind, and sadly, growth ceases. If you want to continue to grow, remain open to learning.

- **GROW.** Growth is a season of its own. It's essential to learn how to respond to the seasons of growth. When the business is booming, some are tempted to expand or invest. While I'm not saying not to investigate these options, I am saying to be mindful that growth is not guaranteed. Making significant investments or moves based solely on the boom of today is not wise. Learning how to bring in the crop without destroying the future growth potential is essential. You must learn how to financially and personally handle successful seasons and the benefits that accompany them.

- **REPRODUCE.** Many get wrapped up in what they are doing and miss the opportunity to lend support to someone coming up behind them. No matter your dream or vision, others are always behind you, attempting to maneuver the roads you have already traveled. You reproduce when you take the time to turn around and invest yourself in their endeavors. When the opportunity comes, don't allow "I'm too busy" to keep you from this season.

So, tell me, what season are you in, and what are you doing within that season? Every season has some specifics you must do to maximize your efforts in that particular time. Determine your season and do what is required.

You are amazing; let your passion burn bright!

> *When you are finished changing, you are finished.* ~ Benjamin Franklin

Now It's Time To Invest

Select one of your endeavors. What season are you in currently?

Describe to yourself what you are doing in that season to prepare yourself for the next season.

Of the seven seasons listed above, is there one you struggle with more than the others? Discuss with yourself the whys.

Are there other seasons in your life? List them; remember, it's your list.

One Step at a Time

When Steve and I visited Paris for the first time, I had no idea what it would take to see *The Mona Lisa*. I assumed the museum would be like the ones in Washington, DC. You take the METRO, get off at a stop within walking distance to the entrance, walk up a few stairs, and there you have it. Let me help all who plan to visit the Louvre Museum in Paris, France. There are stairs, so many stairs, more stairs than I have ever seen connected together. When the lady told us the entrance was "up there," I asked if there was another way. I can laugh now, but there was no laughter that day. About halfway up, my Apple watch announced I had met my goal; as I looked up and saw the stairs still in front of me, I wanted to throw it, but I was too busy using my energy to breathe. We made it to the top. When I saw *The Mona Lisa*, I thought, "For all the stairs I had to climb, this should be a bigger painting." I guess I was still recovering from the physical trauma I had just endured.

Looking back at that adventure, I realize the only way I made it was to focus on the step directly in front of me, not the entire staircase. The same philosophy is true when we approach new ventures, opportunities, and plans we are passionate about; we must take it one step at a time. Yes, you get the big picture, the desired result, but to achieve success, you must have a goal action plan that consists of achievable steps that will lead you to victory. A plan without planning will lead to scattered performance and ultimate unnecessary failure.

Let's look at a basic staircase of five steps.

1. **WRITE IT DOWN.** Your plan may be great, but if you leave it in your mind, it will remain a pipedream. That's why God told Habakkuk to write the vision plainly and clearly. There is something powerful about writing. It inspires me when I read a vision, a plan that began years before, and I see it unfolding before my eyes. Don't limit your notes in writing to the big picture; include step-by-step goals with clear objectives and a goal action plan. Instead of vague generalizations, clear goals will help crystallize your thinking, leading you to tremendous success. When a dream or desire begins to stir, I begin to write; success demands a written plan for achievement.

2. **FOCUS ON ACTIONS, NOT RESULTS.** Your goal action plan should contain the required actions to complete each step. Focus on the actions; the results will automatically occur. For example, if your goal is to lose 40 pounds, step one of your plan would be to exercise 5 days a week. Concentrate on keeping the exercise date with yourself and maximize your exercise sessions. Don't become overwhelmed by what the scale is saying; as you do the actions, eventually, the results will show, and the scale will sing the song you want to hear!

3. **BE CONSISTENT.** Your step-by-step goals are your roadmap to success. I remember growing up when our family traveled the country in the RV. This was before smartphones and GPS; sometimes, we would get off course. Papa would pull out the big book of maps, the Rand McNally, to figure out where we took a wrong turn and get us back on track. To get to our destination, we had to follow the map consistently. You must follow your roadmap and plan to see your passion come to life. Every step you take forward is a step toward fulfilling your dreams, and every detour takes you off the map. Sometimes, I get stuck and faced with an unexpected roadblock; in these times, I reach out to my coach or a support team member. I will always stress the value of a coach and a network of support in your life for success.

4. **LEARN FROM YOUR SETBACKS.** Setbacks are not failures unless you allow them to make you quit; they are classrooms for learners. They provide an opportunity to step back and evaluate. No plan I have made at the beginning of an endeavor has been the plan to usher me into success. Your plan is a living document that's constantly changing, and usually, the cue to change is a setback. One of my mentors, Steve Harvey, said, "Growth is a series of mistakes. That's the only way you learn." If your dream, vision, or plan of passion is worthwhile, expect, accept, and learn from setbacks.

5. **CELEBRATE THE WINS WHEN THEY OCCUR.** Do not waste your life planning the enormous celebration at the end of the plan — the launching of the business or the loss of the total pounds; learn to celebrate the little wins when they happen. You should observe and acknowledge small victories along the way. This ignites my passion to

keep plowing forward. The road to success is like the roads we traveled when I was a little girl, filled with memories and moments that stick with you for a lifetime. If you only focus on getting to the destination, you will miss the value of the journey.

You have a greater capacity for success than you realize. Don't allow untamed zeal and desire for instant gratification to cause you to attempt to run up the stairs. Allow your determination to set you apart as you reach the top. See the big picture, but keep your focus on the next step.

There is no elevator to success, you have
to take the stairs. ~ Zig Ziglar

Now It's Time To Invest

Who do you trust to share your dreams? We know you can't share with everyone; however, there should be someone who you trust to encourage you as you take the steps to success. Write that person's name here and list the reasons and character qualities that make them worthy of your trust.

How do you respond when you cannot achieve something by a specific timeline? Is that the correct way to respond? If not, what are you willing to do to change your approach?

Have critics ever succeeded in discouraging you from going after a goal? What do you do to prevent that from happening again?

Rising Above Negativity

I'm sure you have heard how crabs in a bucket will pull down a crab trying to escape. Do you know why? Their behavior has no ill intent; crabs pull on things when they can't swim. Since there are only other crabs in the bucket, that's what they pull on. When I read that fact, it made sense to me. But I can't understand why people act like crabs trying to pull others down with negative words. It's not like if I become successful, you can't become successful too. There is no limit to the number of people who can be successful. Honestly, there was a time when the crab mentality among humans bothered me. Notice I said, "There was a time"; that's past tense. Now, I don't have time to concern myself with the opinions of others or how they arrived at their conclusion. To get there, I had to learn to rise above negativity.

You probably encounter negative people and situations daily; I know I do. While I can't control the encounters, I can control how I respond and how involved I become.

One of the first things I did to rise above negativity was to ensure I wasn't being negative to myself. There is a difference between analyzing something you did that didn't turn out as well as you planned and being negative, complaining, and pessimistic. The first will help you prepare for the next endeavor; the latter will cause you to be hesitant in the next venture.

Another essential part of rising above negativity is deciding the value you place on what people say. For example, something my husband says carries more weight than what a Facebook "friend" says. If one of the ladies in my circle shares an observation with me, it's more valuable than an Instagram follower's input. I've seen people question their ideas and dreams after a social media warrior fired shots of negativity! For me, I see the comments, and I think, "Who are you again?" If I tried to please everyone and do what everyone thought I should, I would be a crazy woman running around in circles, accomplishing nothing. The way I dress, the color of my hair, the business decisions, marriage tips, child-rearing concerns, names of my businesses, vehicles we drive, how much I share on social media, and on and on — someone seems to have something to say about everything. And yes, sometimes the shots come from the ones you love. Learn to weigh the value of words. I have found that most are not worth a double-read.

Finally, I choose to be different. Galatians 6:7 is true; it says, *"you will always harvest what you plant."* I choose to plant encouragement. I am a cheerleading coach! I love to see people doing their best! Not only will I cheer them on in victory, but I will cheer them up when they feel defeated.

I love to invest in others to help them realize their full potential. I choose to be different. Yes, I choose to be different even to people who have criticized and verbally attacked me in the past. It's not always the easy road, but it is the road I choose to take, and it works for me. I'm determined to be so positive that negative people will see the difference and want to change, or they will walk away.

Life is too short, and my energy is too valuable to wrestle around with the negativity of others. I have victories to win; what about you? Learn to rise above negativity!

No matter where life takes me there will always be someone who's threatened by it. ~ Franchesca Ramsey

Now It's Time To Invest

Do you practice negative and critical self-talk? It's unhealthy, and I venture to say it doesn't leave you excited to get up and try again. Think of ways you can change how you talk to yourself. Brainstorm your thinking session right here.

Are there people close to you who tend to be negative, offering "very strong corrective criticism?" Do you allow what they say to affect you negatively? How do you handle them, and is there a need for change? If so, journal it out here.

The Fire of Passion

Every once in a while, you get a rare moment to redefine yourself. Your moment is now. ~ Shanel Evans, Friend

In the world of business, the people who are most successful are those who are doing what they love. ~ Warren Buffett

Small wins are still won, and the journey is more important than overnight success. ~ Bill Watterson

The dream is free, but the hustle is sold separately. ~ Steve Harvey

The only place where your dream becomes impossible is in your own thinking. ~ Robert H Schuller

The way to get started is to quit talking and begin doing. ~ Walt Disney

There are so many people who will tell you that you can't do this, but you have to make sure that your voice isn't going to be one of them. ~ Pooja Agnihotri

How Do You Handle the Storm?

According to my calendar, I would soon be landing in sunny Orlando, Florida. My day planner was filled with arrangements for my first mega retreat, months of preparation laid before me on paper. However, a storm between here and there canceled everything, and there I sat.

What do you do when a storm interrupts your plans? How do you handle the storms of life?

That day, I quickly discovered that focusing on the storm was a waste of time. Weather channels and apps allowed me to track the storm, but what good would that do? Focusing on the storm was a total waste of my time and energy. Instead, I did the unthinkable; I took advantage of the storm and the white space it created on my normally packed calendar. I used the storm as an opportunity to think and focus on myself.

Since everyone in my world had planned for my absence, I sat quietly and gave thought to myself.

- I considered what I wanted to get out of this new season of adventure and endeavors.
- I mentally dug for more profound clarity and understanding of my vision and purpose.
- I reflected on how far God has brought me and the next level He was leading me into.
- I pondered my expectations at the next level for myself and those who work with me.

As I sat in silence, I realized that one of the things I learned during COVID was to approach the storm differently. Before COVID, the unexpected cancellation or delay of the retreat plans would have sent me into a tailspin, but I learned that while there are situations that I can change, there are facts of life that I must accept. True champions understand storms are facts of life that you must accept, but they also know the storms contain opportunities to improve on the other side.

During that time of reflection, I spent significant time thinking about the "Secret" of my success. Actually, He is not a secret, and if you know anything about me, you know I'm talking about Jesus. He has kept me, my family, and my businesses through every storm. When the storms of life hit, I turn to Him, and during that time of reflection, I recalled how valuable that relationship is to me.

I encourage you when the next storm hits, take time to do the following:

- **REFLECT.** Reflect on where you have been and where you are heading. Evaluate where you are right now and your plans to get from here to there.
- **RENEW.** Renew your thinking. Sometimes, when the storm is over, the best thing you can have is a renewed mindset. As you reflect, give yourself the ok to admit that you have approached something wrong or that there is a better way.
- **RETRAIN.** Retrain yourself and those around you. What you come out of the storm with will require some retraining for you and those around you. Don't be afraid to change. The decision to change something doesn't necessarily mean you were wrong; it might mean there is a better way to succeed now.

As you rise above the storm, you may need a mentor or coach to push you to the next level. Don't be afraid to believe and invest in yourself. Don't fear the changes the storm brings. Don't allow storms to stop you and cause you to return to behaviors that bring negative results. Instead, get over it. Sometimes, you must let the storm pass; just wait it out and let it go. Finally, always remember to pray. Your prayers will create a shelter to keep you in a place where you will be safe and strengthened during the storms of life.

The storm is coming; how will you handle it?

Every storm runs out of rain, just like every dark night turns into day. ~ Gary Allen

Now It's Time To Invest

What is your natural response to the storms of life?

Have you allowed a storm to keep you from accomplishing a goal?

How do you want to handle the next storm in your life?

Do You Remember the Whens or the Wins?

Our memories are wonderful but tricky things. After almost three decades with my husband and raising three children, I'm convinced that memories are also selective, at least in my house. Honestly, selecting or choosing what and how you remember something is not necessarily a terrible characteristic. This week's title has two sides of the coin; let's look at both sides.

Do you remember the whens or the wins? Do you remember who was with you when you started? Do you remember when you were struggling with the startup and the lessons those humble beginnings taught you? Do you remember the value and the process of strengthening that came with navigating those menacing mountains? Do you remember the laughter and prayers that bounced off the walls of that tiny apartment? Likewise, do you remember your wins? The time you won, the time you graduated, the time you were victorious, the time you earned your first dollar or first million dollars, the people that stayed, the mountains you have slayed. I believe there is value in remembering the victories and the struggles, the people who stayed and those who left, the whens and the wins.

Do you remember the whens or the wins? Then, some people remember the whens in a negative or dull light. Let me tell you that pale light will reduce the potential brightness of the connecting areas. They reflect on the struggle and forget the good or wins in the battle. They remember those who have left, not the victories they helped you through. They recall the struggle of menacing mountains but not the faith muscles developed during the process of climbing. They replay the pain, disappointment, loss, and rejection of when and never fully celebrate the wins. They even paint pictures in their heads with yesterday's paint that depict a distorted truth of their when that causes them to bypass a victory celebration.

I recently ran into someone who meant the world to my family and me in years past. When we parted ways, it was not on the best terms. However, through the years, I could never forget the whens. When he encouraged me, gave me advice, cheered me on, made time for my struggles, and celebrated every one of my wins. For years, he was a big part of my whens and wins. The memories were there, and I refused to let them go; they were just as much a positive part of my life as breathing. When I saw him, the great memories returned. Our conversation was brief, but during those few moments, I was reminded of his impact of love on my whens and wins. The one thing I held onto that blessed me most was when he said, "I am proud of you!" That was a win from when to add to my treasure chest.

Remember the whens and the wins, and keep everything in perspective. It's natural to remember the bad, but make it a point to remember more of the good.

Memories play a very confusing role. They make us laugh when we remember the times we cried but make us cry when we remember the times we laughed! ~ Unknown

Now It's Time To Invest

Take this week and journal memories. Remember the whens and the wins and celebrate both here.

Stay Motivated

In 2006, I asked one of my friends to help me prepare for tax season. I purchased this new system in 2005 to help me record and keep up with all my expenses. However, I didn't stay motivated long enough after the purchase to begin using the thing. Each day, I told myself today, today, ok for real today, but something always got in my way, or I should say I allowed things to get in my way. So, at the beginning of 2006, I ushered her into a room filled with various bags that contained all my previous year's receipts. The result of my lack of motivation was stuffed in bags. It's a true story; I can laugh about it now, and while it was more than 16 years ago, I still remember the lesson.

Motivation never seems to last for long. It's not that we don't know what to do; it's getting ourselves to do what we know we should do consistently. That's the problem. Here are some ways I've found to reignite my motivation fire.

- **VISUALIZE YOUR SUCCESS.** Make use of that great imagination and allow yourself to see the project done if you stay motivated.

- **DECLUTTER YOUR WORK AREA.** Ouch! Right? Sometimes, you need motivation just to declutter. However, providing a clutter-free space will allow you to focus on the assignment, not the mess around you.

- **AVOID WORRYING ABOUT THE THINGS THAT DON'T MATTER.** Stay focused on the assignment, not the other things that don't matter. Blocking out notifications and phone calls for a while will help you in this area. I don't know about you, but one "ting" from my phone can cost me hours.

- **SET VERY SHORT-TERM GOALS AND CELEBRATE YOUR ACHIEVEMENTS.** Short-term may be one day or one week, you call it. But let the celebration be in line with the accomplishment. Don't get a large piece of chocolate cake to celebrate your first day at the gym.

- **WATCH THE MOTIVATION VACUUMS IN YOUR LIFE.** What things, people, situations, and locations suck out your motivation to stay on task? For me, it was being physically located in the office with members of my executive staff. I needed a private place to stay focused and not get wrapped up in something I had delegated.

- **KEEP TABS ON YOUR PROCRASTINATING SELF.** Watch yourself and your excuses for procrastinating. Don't give yourself an unlimited pass to talk yourself out of doing what you planned to do.

- **LIST THE ADVANTAGES AND THE CONSEQUENCES.** Visiting the advantages of reaching your goals and the consequences of allowing your lack of motivation to derail you will sometimes motivate you to stay the course you've charted.

- **REMIND YOURSELF OF YOUR PAST SUCCESSES AS YOU STICK TO THE TASK.** In other words, encourage yourself and pat yourself on the back. Break out the pom poms and cheer you on to victory. During some of my most challenging times, I found a song that reminded me of God's faithfulness in the past and the achievements He led me to was a great encourager. Songs like I Trust You by James Fortune were the motivation I needed to see me through some dark days!

- **JUST GET STARTED; MOTIVATION WILL COME.** Sometimes, jumping in and starting is the only way to get motivated. Put on some good music and get going. Put the phone on silent for a little while. Before you know it, the mountain before you will become a little hill, and seeing that will motivate you to keep going.

- **SHARE YOUR NEED TO GET MOTIVATED.** Share it with someone in one of your circles who will hold you accountable. There is nothing like a good friend who will hold you to your word. Sometimes, the motivation to keep going is just so you can joyfully say, "Yes, I did!"

Don't be too hard on yourself when you sense your motivation running low. No one's motivation is set on 100% one hundred percent of the time; it's temporary, and that's why giving it a jump start every now and then is necessary. Motivation is the juice that allows us to get things done. Knowing how to squeeze the fruit to get the juice at will is a powerful skill.

I think I can. I think I can. I think I can. I know
I can. ~ The Little Engine That Could

Now It's Time To Invest

List the three greatest motivation vacuums in your life. What's a way to work past them?

Is your motivation tank on low right now? Choose four of the suggestions mentioned in this section and discuss with yourself if they would be tools for you. Brainstorm your discussion below.

Suggestion 1 —

Suggestion 2 —

Suggestion 3 —

Suggestion 4 —

Let's Go!

I struggle to control my facial expression when I encounter my Costco, Sam's Club, and BJ followers. These are those "loyal" followers who meet me anywhere and open their conversation with a line something like this.

I have been following you.
I use your tips.
I should have joined your coaching program 2 years ago.
I see you doing big things.
I should have attended one of your workshops or conferences.
I don't know how you do it.

These are the type of followers who shop at the club member warehouse stores for the samples and only on the free membership day. They never buy the whole meal or purchase a membership; they just move from a free sample table to a free sample table. They never get full, and they are never satisfied. However, they keep coming back, looking for something FREE. Using the same temporary card. Until they are stopped at the door because their temporary membership has EXPIRED!!!!

I want to encourage all club member browsers to stop living off the samples and join a membership where you can enjoy ALL THE BENEFITS!!! When you become a member, you get access to so much more than occasional free samples. Early entry, special discounts, the employees know you by name, and you get access to all the upcoming events and bonus items.

Don't waste your time on social media worrying about what everyone else has going on. My question to you is, *what's going on with you?* Let me be honest; I used to do some of the same things. I would look at every person on my timeline and the timeline of others, picking from the tidbits they dropped, attempting to gather the fullness of what they were saying from the bits and pieces. I would compare me and my results to them and their results, and I always seemed to come up short. Oh, I experienced a level of success but not the fullness I knew was possible. Yes, I was there; I know what I'm talking about, and I know the frustration that comes from nibbling on a sample when your heart screams for the whole thing!

Finally, I decided I could be doing so much more than watching other people obtain super success in their area of pursuit. I stopped picking up the samples and began purposefully pursuing my dreams and visions. I started making vision boards, attending conferences, and getting various certifications that would allow me in rooms I never considered possible. I shifted my focus from what everyone else was doing to me and what I've been called to accomplish! I stopped settling for the samples. I knew the passion that stirred inside me, and I knew I would never see the success

I dreamed of watching other people on social media and munching on their free samples.

What is your passion? What is it that you sniff around but never really sink your teeth into? What are you afraid of? What's holding you back? LET'S GO! If the time is not now to step out and pursue the next level of what you are working on, then when? Surely not tomorrow because we all know tomorrow is that elusive day that never comes; tomorrow is the procrastinator's favorite deadline.

Things began to change once I stopped sampling and started actively investing in myself and my passion. Now, I coach men and women as they endeavor to achieve their NEXT LEVEL in all areas of life, not just entrepreneurship. I have 30 years of experience as an entrepreneur, and I have made many mistakes. And while I have considered it many times, the one thing I never did was GIVE UP!

So, to those who are "loyal" followers sampling the free stuff but not investing in yourself, no more free samples; it's time for YOU to invest in YOURSELF! You are worth it!

LET'S GO!

The best investment you can make is an investment in yourself. The more you learn, the more you'll earn. ~ Warren Buffett

Now It's Time To Invest

Who do you secretly or openly follow picking up the free tips? Is this really the best you can do in pursuit of your dreams?

What is one thing that you can and will do this week to invest in your passion? Detail your plan here.

By the end of the week, tell yourself how it felt to work on you and your passion. Be clear with yourself, so if you forget how great it felt, you will be reminded with your own words! LET'S GO

Don't Quit

You can't be afraid to fail if you've never even tried first. ~ Stephen L. Brown, Jr., Son

Don't let your mind stop you. ~ Steve Harvey

Failure is not the opposite of success it is part of success. ~ Unknown

Growth is in a series of mistakes. That's the only way you learn. ~ Steve Harvey

Instead of letting your hardships and failures discourage or exhaust you, let them inspire you. ~ Michelle Obama

Nothing will work unless you do. ~ Maya Angelou

People often say that motivation doesn't last. Well, neither does bathing—that's why we recommend it daily. ~ Zig Ziglar

Success is not final, failure is not fatal: it is the courage to continue that counts. ~ Winston Churchill

Purpose

Walking in MY Purpose

What is your purpose? What would be left if you were stripped of everything you do, assignments, and titles? I define purpose as what you are called to do, which is often your passion. Years ago, I realized MY purpose is to help people discover that it's ok to be their authentic selves. My sister, Nikea, says I'm like a midwife; I help people give birth to their dreams. I like that, and it fits me well. Looking back, from the beginning, it's what I have done, from the children in the daycare to the multi-million-dollar corporate executives; ultimately, my burning desire is to see people become their authentic selves, walking fully in their purpose.

To walk in your purpose, you must first discover, know, understand, and handle your purpose well. It stands to reason that you cannot walk in something you do not know. For the record, no one can tell you what you were created to do. As a coach, I help others discover their purpose, but I cannot tell them what it is. I could not tell my children their purpose; they had to make that discovery themselves.

If you do not know your purpose, sit for a while with yourself. Close out the voices that tell you what you should do; this is not a conference call. Create your personal vision statement, line out anything you do not love, and highlight your strengths and achievements. Before long, you should notice some things standing out, some themes repeating themselves. You will begin to connect your dots.

Once you know your purpose, seek to understand it for yourself before you run and share it with the world. How is your purpose currently intertwined in your life? What are additional avenues you can pursue to understand, work in, and perfect the placement of purpose in your life? Journal, journal, journal. Even if it doesn't make sense right now, write it down. I'm like my mother; I have notes written on the back of envelopes, napkins, and books, and I have journals; oh, do I have journals. Last week, I read an article I wrote over a year ago. Let me share it with you:

I have always been a fan of journals. Small ones, big ones, and, of course, journals that have bling are my favorites.

Journals are a way I stay organized but also a way for me to track my thoughts, dreams, and goals I need to accomplish during the year. I also include prayers and things I'm grateful for as well.

Journal writing can be therapeutic and a way to connect with your authentic self.

Are you journaling in 2021?

If you don't journal, I encourage you to begin, especially as you seek to understand your purpose and obtain a higher level of success.

As you learn to know and understand your purpose, ensure you include learning how to handle your purpose. Here are a few pointers I've learned, some the hard way.

- My time is my most valuable asset; therefore, I manage my time for success.
- Not everyone values my time, but I always do.
- I create time to do the things I love and need to do. Everything doesn't require my hands.
- I focus on things I can control.
- I focus on what is important at the moment.
- Time away from my work is just as important as time at my work.

As I walk in MY purpose, because I am confident that I am doing what I am called to do, I've learned that no matter how many challenges I face, I keep going, moving forward, and rising above the challenges. Walking in MY purpose is ingrained into the core of who I am. It is often the explanation of why I do what I do. I own MY purpose; it is mine, and no one told me or forced me to walk this walk. I discovered MY purpose, and the passion explains it all to me.

What is your purpose? Make that discovery, and you will find the match that lights your passion.

A woman who walks in purpose doesn't have to
chase people or opportunities. Her light causes people
and opportunities to pursue her. ~ Unknown

Now It's Time To Invest

Do you journal? If not, why? Are you one of those people who overthink journalling? You do not have to write well, write every day, spell all the words correctly, structure the sentences, or use complete sentences. It is your tool for now and for later. Consider giving it another try if you have put it down. This time, allow yourself to be free in your journal.

What is your purpose? Start your brainstorming here. If you are uncertain, use some of these tips or find some of your own to discover your purpose.

Consider the people who are drawn to you. What about you draws them? Write names and what drew them. What theme do you see forming from your analysis?

Are You Hiding from Success?

Before you say, "That's a silly question. Who hides from success?" Take a moment to consider the question, read a little further, and give your answer a bit more thought.

The definition of success is a flourishing and favorable conclusion, the accomplishment of an aim or purpose. Success is not a destination; it's a process. Like climbing a ladder, reaching each rung marks victory as the next rung is before you. In considering success, don't limit your thinking to financial aspirations. The desire to succeed is not limited to one area of your life, no matter what you do. Whether you are a chief home officer, aka stay-at-home mom, the president of a multi-million-dollar company, a college student, a new bride, or an entrepreneur, the desire to succeed is natural, expected, and necessary.

Many, at the beginning of an endeavor, have crazy plans for radical success. However, somewhere in the process, faced with unexpected challenges, when the actual cost of success is unveiled, their words continue to speak of radical achievement, but inside, a private struggle begins to brew.

The battle with this internal opponent causes them to back off, power down, and hide from the most incredible level of victory possible in their endeavors. Notice I said, "greatest level of victory?" In other words, they achieve a level of success, but the fullness of absolute success remains out of reach. And somewhere in their heart, they know it.

Allow me to pull back the curtain on the internal opposition that causes many to accept mediocrity, preventing them from achieving the radical triumphs of their dreams. His name is fear. As a coach to many, I started researching why some clients shift from earnestly pursuing their dreams to a different set of behaviors. For example, they struggle to make decisions, talk without follow-through action, leave projects undone, and have an excuse to cover the new trend that doesn't match the initial zeal. The words they speak are the same, but the heart is missing.

I was surprised to discover that fear of succeeding is so common that it has clinical names such as success anxiety, success phobia, and achievemephobia. People fear leaving people behind as they succeed, new responsibilities, more complicated living, isolation, and failure, for example.

Fear of failure and fear of success. There is an account in the Bible where several men faced a life-threatening decision and came to a conclusion: if we stay here, we will die, and if we go forward, we might die. Ultimately, they went forward, obtaining great victory for themselves and others. The same decision presents itself before everyone who is taunted by fear. While the death will not be physical, the regret will be great as the dreamer, stopped by fear, watches their dreams die.

Let's relook at and redefine our understanding of failure. I genuinely believe there are only two ways to fail in a negative sense. First, if you never start the thing that you are supposed to begin. Second, if you quit when you should keep going, think about that. I know it will challenge many because people have been taught to attach the negative and terminal label of failure to many moments in life as if that is the end. This is my take on failure and what I attempt to encourage my clients, family, and friends with.

- **FAILURE IS EDUCATIONAL.** It's my lifelong philosophy. I don't fail because I don't quit, and I don't fail to start; I learn. Think of a baby learning to walk. When they fall, do you say they failed? No, you say they are learning. I learned what didn't work, how not to approach something, and what not to do. It is not the end; it's an opportunity to back up, learn something and continue moving forward.
- **FAILURE IS COMMON.** As we learn and grow, it is common to miss the mark and not always select the correct course of action. However, attaching a negative end-of-the-road period to the setback is self-sabotaging. Yep, I failed at this approach or attempt, but this is not a failure, and neither am I.
- **FAILURE IS TEMPORARY.** Thomas Edison, who was told he was too stupid to learn anything, experienced many setbacks as an inventor, but he never failed in his ultimate goal of creating the light bulb and

over 1,000 other things. Being rejected over 26 times as a writer did not stop Theodor Geisel from continuing to pursue his dreams, and that's a great thing for us. Can you imagine life without the well-loved Dr. Suess? The only way failure is permanent is if you quit.

While you are attaining success, you are never completely free of fear. Achievement always involves change, and all change involves some apprehension. You might genuinely desire success, but if the feelings of fear outweigh the positive feelings in your mind, progress will be slow and challenging.

To eliminate fears of failure and success, two of the best things you can do is to identify and examine your fears and use your support team. When you identify and analyze your fears, you often discover that the "boogie man" is not as terrifying as you created in your mind. I believe that of the two, the most powerful is your support team. If you are honest, they will strengthen and cheer you forward. They will help you push past the fear and encourage you to continue and reach higher heights.

I encourage you not to hide from your success; the world is waiting for you and your gift.

What would you do if you weren't afraid?" ~ Steve Harvey

Now It's Time To Invest

One of the things that assists me in staying focused and not being distracted by internal struggles is a vision board. If you have one, display it in a visible place. If you don't have a vision board, consider creating one.

Think of a goal that you'd like to achieve. Then, take 20-30 minutes and answer the question: "What will happen if I succeed?" Write down everything you can think of — both good and bad consequences of achieving your goal. It's important to take at least 20 minutes to answer the question. Your early answers are likely to be superficial. Simply keep writing for at least 20 minutes. Put down everything that comes to mind. Nothing is too silly or too small. If, after 20 minutes, you're still getting good stuff, then keep on going.

Do the same exercise tomorrow or the next day, only write a different goal you would like to achieve, and don't look at your previous journal entry. After you finish the second part, check for consistency in your concerns or fears.

Are You on Your Way?

Have you ever talked to someone passionate about their ideas and plans? You could see them bubble with excitement as they laid out their vision like well-rehearsed lines from a movie they had seen 40 times. Listening, they had it together, standing on go mode and ready to launch. However, you knew the passionate one was talking the same talk they had talked for years. They craved success, longed to step off the launching pad, could feel the pull into the new and unknown, and yet remained stuck.

In a teaching, I heard Dr. Myles Munroe say *"The wealthiest place in the world is not the gold mines of South America or the oil fields of Iraq or Iran. They are not the diamond mines of South Africa or the banks of the world. The wealthiest place on the planet is just down the road. It is the cemetery. There lie buried companies that were never started, inventions that were never made, bestselling books that were never written, and masterpieces that were never painted. In the cemetery is buried the greatest treasure of untapped potential."*

What causes people to live and die with a dream burning in their hearts? One thing that stops many visions from ever becoming a reality is limiting beliefs. The voices inside of your head that scream louder than your dreams. The doubting voice that lists the reasons your vision will never work, and usually, the list is filled with "you." You are not smart enough. You have never done anything like this. You need more time to prepare. You failed the last time you tried something new. You only have a high school diploma. You will lose. You will be the big joke of the family when you fail. You don't have the finances. You are not that talented. You need a real job. You should stop dreaming. The voices keep you craving success and stuck in your own limiting beliefs.

Can you relate to what I'm saying? I believe, to some degree, we can all relate personally to thoughts that attempt to limit our success by attacking our beliefs and confidence. Where does all of this come from? What happened that caused us to doubt? I'm convinced that two primary sources feed doubt: society and people.

Look at television, read the news, and check out social media; you'll find plenty of reasons to doubt yourself and your dreams. The labels and limitations are endless. If you are not careful, you will consume more of society's messages of failure than of abilities to succeed.

The second is people. People plant seeds of failure that take root and bloom when dreams enter. Hear me now; while some people are mean and intend to hurt and destroy, not everyone who planted failure in your memory bank did so out of spitefulness. Some were speaking from the depths of their own heart of failure. However, regardless of the intention, the potential to cause internal limiting beliefs remains the same.

Words, labels, and limitations are sent like destructive missiles to restrict your success and come at any time in your life. I recall a personal situation that happened to me when I was enjoying the success of my dreams and visions. The verbal attack caught me off guard and honestly caused me to question myself and others around me. Yes, this is Coach Nicole being transparent. But it's important to me that you know doubtful thoughts that aim to destroy your purpose are sent after everyone.

How do you get unstuck or prevent getting stuck? After all, we all want to succeed.

1. **GUARD YOUR HEART.** Proverbs 4:23 instructs us, *"Above all else, guard your heart, for everything you do flows from it."* You can't control what people say, but you can control what you give value and life to. As well you can control what you listen to. Refuse negative talk or conversation that is counterproductive to your success to continue in your presence. Would you sit in a group and sip poison to keep from hurting someone's feelings? Exactly, get up and walk away. Remember to shield what you watch and listen to as you guard your heart. You have the remote control in your hand; if it's feeding your limiting beliefs about yourself and your plan to succeed, click the off button.

2. **THINK ABOUT WHAT YOU THINK.** There are thoughts, mindsets, and opinions that we have had since childhood. We don't know why we think

or say it except "it's always been that way." Why do you think that way? Who told you that you were not enough? Challenge your thinking and dispose of the garbage.

3. **USE YOUR CIRCLE OF PROTECTION.** You know I believe big in my circles. They encourage, strengthen, and, at times, protect. They protect me from me when I want to quit, when an unexpected attack hits me, and when limiting belief tries to slip in. To succeed as an entrepreneur, you need circles of protection. Your circle is your lifeline.

4. **SPEAK AFFIRMATIONS.** You talk to yourself more than anyone else, so why not speak positively to yourself? Be intentional and speak encouraging words that affirm the truth about yourself.

5. **BELIEVE IN YOURSELF.** If you do not believe in yourself, no one else will. However, if you believe in yourself, no one's doubt in you will make a difference in your success. Believe in you!

Don't allow limiting beliefs in yourself to keep you stuck! I refuse to live or die with an untapped dream burning in my heart. I refuse to be full of talk and never launch! You have dreams! Let's go! It's time to satisfy your craving for success; it's time to get unstuck as you venture into success! You got this.

One of the lessons that I grew up with was to always stay true to yourself and never let what somebody else says distract you from your goals. — Michelle Obama

Now It's Time To Invest

Is there an area that you are stuck in where you can connect your thoughts to limited belief in yourself? If so, journal where the belief came from, and specifically, the erroneous ideas that have you stuck or struggling.

Who are the members of your circle of protection?

Do you believe in yourself 100%? Why or why not?

Stand Firm

I love word art! I have frames, pictures, plaques, boards, pillows, and signs everywhere I live and work. The words speak passion, encouragement, reminders, strength, and peace. They remind readers to laugh, breathe, appreciate, love, live, and capture the moments. The look sparkles and blings to catch the eye, and the words capture the heart, causing you to pause in the moment. At *Nikki B. Jewels Boutique*, we are accustomed to patrons staying in the restroom a little longer than usual. They come out smiling, commenting on the word art experience they just encountered. We have seen portions of our restroom "featured" on social media. I love word art, and I've learned that what it does for me, it also does for others.

Words are powerful; they have the strength to build up or destroy — give life or kill and cast hope or despair. Before I started buying word art, I created my own, so to speak. I would write notes on any piece of paper handy; I know I get that from my Mom. The back of an envelope turned into a place to pen plans or encouragement.

Have you heard the saying, *"In a world where you can be anything, be yourself?"* That speaks volumes of encouragement, hope, and promise to me. Advertisements, social media, peer pressure, misguided personal desires, movies, and music scream at us to change who we are to become like someone else. Unfortunately, many are doing just that with plastic surgery, job changes, personality altering, eating, shopping, going to places, changing the way we talk and the people we surround ourselves with, and applying to certain schools, all in an attempt to be like someone else. Years ago, while watching others attempt to transform into someone they are not, I discovered that becoming someone else requires losing who I am. For me, that is not an acceptable option.

I have decided to be myself in a world where I can be anything! To come to that conclusion, I had to understand that my unique self makes me valuable; your unique self makes you valuable. Would you accept if someone offered you $500 for the $50,000 you have in the bank? Would you think for a moment about the possibility? Would you be tempted to make the trade if they put the $500 in an eye-catching envelope? Of course not; that would be crazy. When people trade who they are for someone else, they trade down.

I am always who I am. I have learned that I am best at being myself. Oh, sure, if I could have talked to God before He made me, I would have requested a few changes to His plan, but I didn't get that chance, so I am who I am, and I'm going to stand firm in that. Learning to be someone else would take too much work; I have no time for that. I would be uncomfortable dressing like someone else; life is too short to be uncomfortable for no purpose. My determination and drive for success — I like that about me. I'm not wired to sit back and wait for success to find me; I'm going to capture it. Being my true self in all settings and situations does not frighten me; it is ultimately empowering and relaxing as I stand firm in Nicole L. Brown.

I realize everyone doesn't like me, and I'm ok with that truth. Here's another fact: no matter who I tried to become, everyone would not like me, but most importantly, I would not like myself. In 2007, Kirk Franklin wrote *I Like Me*. The lyrics began with *"I like me. You me like? Cause I like me. Do you like me? See, I like me, 'cause He likes me. God likes me."* He then pointed out some of what could be labeled as faults or defects, but he stood firm on the truth that he likes himself.

Stand firm on who God has created and called you to be. Embrace and enjoy who you are, doing what you are called to do. You are amazing, you are unique, you are valuable, and you are you! Stand firm in that; the world needs you, not a photocopy of someone else.

My job, I realized, was to be myself, to speak as myself. And so I did. ~ Michelle Obama

Now It's Time To Invest

Are there situations or people in your life that cause you to consider becoming someone other than yourself, even for a short period? If so, consider why and if you're really all right with the double personality living. Journal it out here.

Have you ever pushed past the real you to fit into a group that you knew you earnestly did not belong to? Journal your thoughts here.

Seasons Change, and So Do We

Years ago, the Sam's Club in my area made significant changes in their store. I hated it! Why did they change what was not broken? I knew where everything was in that store; I helped other shoppers locate products. They should have put me on the payroll; instead, they changed everything familiar to me. Their new look made my life difficult; that was how I felt.

Change can be challenging; it's made more difficult by our approach and mindset as it applies to the differences. I have learned a few things: change is inevitable in every area of our lives, and absolutely no season stays forever.

Look at Virginia's weather; very subtle leaves begin to change around August, daylight shortens, and temperatures drop as we slowly transition into fall. As that seasonal change occurs, we are forced to change what we wear.

Like it or not, families and their dynamics change. The baby becomes a toddler, goes to school, graduates from college, gets married, and moves to another part of the world. Steve and I have been married for more than 27 years, and let me tell you, we have weathered some seasons and grown through some changes, inside and outside. In our family, we have had the opportunities to celebrate life as we've made room for a new baby and celebrate the life of members we had to learn how to live without.

As I reflect on 30 years in business, I can tell you that change also found me there. I have seen staff members come and go, changed locations, changed logos three times, altered my business plans, and continuously adjusted my goals. I've learned to let go and, at other times, learned to hold on all because of changing seasons.

Look back at your life; some of you were single and are now married, married, and now divorced, married and now widows, employees, and now employers. Good and bad, like it or not, the seasons have been and will always continue to change in small and great ways. How have you handled the season changes? If you're like most people, sometimes you did great, and others, well, not so great.

Is there a way to become more consistent in embracing the seasons in your family, marriage, business, ministry, and health? I believe so; let's look at a few methods.

- **IT'S OK.** Seasons are going to change. Know, understand, and be ok with that truth. I admit some will be more emotionally, financially, or physically challenging than others, but the quicker you accept it, the sooner you will move forward or through the change.
- **DISCOVER JOY IN THE CHANGE.** As much as possible, enjoy the new season; embrace and look for the positive. So many dread their 50th birthday. I found somewhere around 50, I stopped tolerating things and holding on to what I should let go of. I guess you could say I embraced my 50 like a boss!
- **FOCUS ON NOW.** Focus on the season and know when the transition is occurring. If you put your energy into longing for winter or anticipating summer, you will miss the beauty and opportunities for growth in spring.
- **DO YOU NEED TO CHANGE?** Ask questions of yourself. What does this change require of me? Challenge yourself in your purpose and plan for the new season. Just as winter clothes will not work in the summer, you must plan for the changes your new season mandates.
- **IS IT TIME TO REBUILD?** Rebuild where there is a need. Check your business, your blueprint, your staff, your marketing approach, your décor, your approach, your relationships, and check yourself. Some changes will require you to rebuild. Often, we do not achieve the success intended because we take the old blueprint to the new location. It seems easier to keep what wasn't broken. But like Sam's Club, you must understand that just because it's not broken doesn't mean it's the current plan for the greatest success.

- **EMBRACE YOUR CURRENT SEASON.** No matter what season you're in or what event caused the shift, it's ok to find joy and peace that comes when you embrace and get all you can from the new season. To be in this season, what do you have to do, what must you give up, and what should you start? Little is worse than living outside of your season.

Seasons will change. Do not let fear of change stop you. Imagine if the seed in the ground allowed fear to stop its growth. Come on, girl, bust through the dirt! You can do it! {*Insert personal pompoms and a cheer!*}

There is a right time for everything
~ Ecclesiastes 3:1 (TLB)

Now It's Time To Invest

What change have you been resisting or dragging your feet in accepting?

What are you willing to do to embrace a change you have resisted?

Who from your circle will you be completely transparent with concerning your decision?

By what date will you contact them?

I See It!

I get excited at the end of every year, and my creative juices get cranked up! It's the time of the year I jump into preparing for my annual 2-day *Next Level Vision Board Party*! I know the people who attend have a fantastic time, but I don't think they realize how much I look forward to this event. By the end of the *party*, I'm set and focused on the year before me. I've spent two days away from everyday life, concentrating on my vision and goals for the year ahead; it fires up my passion and determination. The atmosphere is charged with excitement and anticipation as passion, purpose, and possibilities replace doubt, fear, and uncertainty. The event culminates with each participant designing their vision board. It's incredible to see the creative passion flow from the heart to the board after spending 48 hours in intimate contact with their vision and others of like mind! It is a moment when they say to themselves, *"I see it!"*

If you want to accomplish your vision, keeping it before your eyes is vital. If you don't believe me, consider the resolutions you made at the beginning of the year. How many have you worked toward or accomplished? How many do you remember? Most of you are drawing a blank or looking for that sheet of paper to answer the question. Preparing and creating a vision board keeps your vision alive and working in you. Through the process, you define and align your vision with motivating images and words that will energize, encourage, and inspire you through the year as you work toward success.

A vision board has powerful potential. The preparation process forces you to decide and refine your vision. After completion, it lets you see and give mental attention to your vision daily. That daily review sensitizes you to opportunities that aid in achieving your vision.

In preparing to create your dream board, don't reduce its importance to a craft project; it's so much more than that. Crafts, once completed, get pushed to the back of the closet, where they are rendered useless and forgotten. Just as crucial, don't expand its scope to a dream board. A vision board is for short-term visions, 6 to 12 months, while a dream board is more about your bucket list and the long-term desired goals. Placing your long-term dreams on a short-term board will potentially leave you frustrated when, at the end of the year, it will seem like you've accomplished less than you thought was possible.

The value of a vision board is not limited to those in business. If you are living and breathing, you should have a vision for your life. One of my favorite scriptures, Proverbs 29:18, states, *"Where there is no vision, the people perish."* Another version says, *"Without vision, people will stumble all over themselves."* Having a vision allows you to set your plans for success, and a vision board helps you to stay focused as you pursue victory.

To create your vision board, you must first decide what you want to be, do, and have in the coming year. Deciding and refining your vision may take a few days and several sheets of paper, but that's fine; it's a process. As you refine your vision, take time to envision what success looks like in each area and put an image to your vision.

Now that you have the mental vision board, it is time to bring it to the physical. How you make your board and what materials you use is your choice; the sky is the limit. Your goal in this stage is to ensure that each picture, word, symbol, and clip speaks to you. I suggest you select the prominent place to display your board and create a size your location can accommodate. Have fun as you prepare your board, dream, and get excited. It's not a competition; just as you don't compare to anyone else, neither does your vision board.

Once your board is complete, daily interaction with it is the next step. You must be vigilant in this step; don't allow time to lead you off course. Hang it in a prominent place. Spend time daily looking at your board, giving life to the success depicted on the board. In the morning and every evening, spend time looking and thinking about what you see. Go through each area on your board and let the time you invest fan the flames and passion of determination. Take a picture of your board to keep on your phone.

Let the plans come alive. No matter where you are, your vision is a part of your life.

Don't allow the vision to stay on the board. As you view it daily, begin to add action to the passion being fanned within your heart. Nothing will happen until you act. You will notice opportunities as you use your board daily; don't waste the chances. Allow the burning passion to move you into action.

Clients have asked me if they should share or keep their boards private. It is your choice. I only offer this small piece of advice; I got it from one of my mentors, Steve Harvey. *"You can't tell big dreams to small-minded people."* Be careful with whom you share your board or your vision, for that matter. Everyone will not favor your vision, and many will want to inject their ideas into it. However, remember it wasn't a conference call when the vision was birthed in your heart. At whatever stage you share your vision, stand firm. Your vision may sound crazy, but as Pastor Mike Todd so eloquently put it, *"It's Crazy Until it Happens."*

If you are looking for an easy way to breathe more fire and passion into your vision, look no further. It's time to work on that vision board.

Cherish your visions and your dreams as they are
the children of your soul, the blueprints of your
ultimate achievements. ~ Napoleon Hill

Now It's Time To Invest

If you have never made a board, today is a great day to start. If you still have the same board from three years ago, it's time for an update. If you have completed your annual board, ask yourself if you are spending the time that you should with your board. If not, let's get it done.

Busy But Are You Productive?

I'm so busy! "I AM VERY BUSY!" We hear it all the time, and yes, each of us has said it at one time or another. But my question is, busy at what? Busy at work or busy at nothing? I have discovered there is a difference between busy and productive people.

Busy people continuously exert energy and effort to work hard, while productive people work hard and smart, producing results. They plan with goals that lead them to complete the project before them.

Busy people drown their time and attention in minor details, even stopping in the process to ask the opinions of others. On the other hand, the productive person maintains their focus on the goal, allowing the minor details to work out during the process.

Busy people say "yes" to everything, but when evening comes, they rarely have accomplished much. Productive people understand they have the power of choice. They choose to accept an assignment consciously, aware that some things accepted will only be a distraction to their established goals. The productive person has no problem saying, "No, I'm focused on a goal and can't do that."

I must laugh at myself in this. I have decided to clean out and organize my closet annually. I always begin the same way: dump everything in the middle of the floor and start from there. At some point, I get thirsty, so I head downstairs for a bottle of water and see the dishes in the sink; there are only a few. Well, like I tell my children, you can't wash dishes without wiping down the counters; everyone knows that. On my way back to my project pile, I grab items that need to go upstairs and put them away. As I head back to the closet, I realize I'm thirsty. At the end of the day, I'm tired, knowing I've done a lot, as I look at the giant pile looking back at me.

There is always a hot new trend that is better than the last. Busy people tend to jump on every new craze, desperate for a way to accomplish something in less time, as they seek tools to free them from the cycle of being busy. Productive people evaluate the pros and cons of everything to answer the questions: Does it fit my schedule? Will it add to my goals? Can I sustain it? The productive-minded individual knows everything hot and new is not for them.

I can't help but think about the diets and weight loss systems that flood the market, many of which I admit I have tried. I lost 30 pounds in one of the hot new diet trends I tried, and all 30 pounds found their way back home. Why? It didn't fit my lifestyle; therefore, it wasn't sustainable. On the other hand, this year, I made some significant lifestyle changes. I decided on changes that I could sustain. The results have been amazing, and my goals are being accomplished!

We have times when we're so busy doing nothing and completing nothing that we accomplish nothing. In those moments, we must slow down, get honest with ourselves, and change the flow.

If you are in a season of life that is busier and less productive, here are a few tips to make the shift.

- Decide what is essential.
- Keep your goal in mind. Subtle distractions are enticing, and they are everywhere.
- Stop adding more than you can handle to your list of things to do.
- Remember, reaching your goals takes time and focus and will require your "no."
- People may not appreciate that they can't convince you to jump on and connect to their passion; remain focused on your lane.
- Include your team and cheerleaders in your decisions; they will help you stay on track.

Enjoy the success that will come from the refocused, productive you.

Don't confuse activity with productivity. Many people are simply busy being busy. ~ Robin Sharma

Now It's Time To Invest

What are some of your biggest distractions?

What are three things you will do this week to eliminate some of the busyness in your life?

What is at least one of those three things you will endeavor to sustain for the next 21 days? What is your simple plan to incorporate this into your life?

Don't Give Up on Your Dreams

My husband Steve has always dreamed of seeing the Eiffel Tower, visiting the Louvre Museum, eating at a sidewalk café, and experiencing the romantic bridges of Paris, France. It wasn't my dream; it has always been his dream. In 2022, he and I did something that many never take the opportunity to accomplish — we experienced a dream come true.

Everyone continuously goes through the process of dreaming. The problem is that most of us talk ourselves out of the dream. Before it has time to grow into the possible, we kill our desire, stuffing it into the hidden corners of what could never happen. We determine it is too big, too expensive, out of our league, or we pollute the possibility with negative talk about ourselves: not smart, talented, or educated enough. Then, to further doom what could and should be, we surround ourselves with a circle of people who water our seeds of disbelief, choking out the growth of a dream meant to be.

Please don't give up on your dreams! No matter what dream burns in your heart, don't give up. You can do whatever you set your mind and heart to; it just takes some planning, preparation, mindset adjustments, and determination to stick to it until it happens.

Be bold, step toward your dream, and begin by writing it out, planning, or creating a vision board. Ok, the plan may change as situations change, but you must start somewhere, so start right here.

Give life to your dream by putting action to the plan. If your goal will take finances, start your savings plan. Don't talk yourself out of it because today, your finances are low. Start with $10 a week; you may have to give up something to reach that. Ask yourself, how important is my dream? If it's losing weight, maybe you can't go to the gym now, but you can walk around your house, set your timer to remind you to drink more water and choose to omit something unhealthy from your diet. It's all about planning; if you want it, you can do it!

Consider your circle of cheerleaders, are they cheerleaders or nay-sayers? I have discovered that not everyone knows how to encourage, and not everyone wants to see you succeed. Some don't mean to be negative; they are just accustomed to evaluating everything by their short measuring stick of possibilities. Your dream challenges their definition of possible. That's why it's your dream. To accomplish your dream, you must learn to ignore the negative talk while loving the negative speaker.

You are too close to give up! Challenges and disruptions are meant to cause you to give up; don't let them win. I remember once when my daycare was in my basement. I faced so much opposition from our neighbors I was ready to quit. For years, no matter what I did, they fought, plotted, and schemed to shut me down. One day, the battle ended suddenly, and I was still standing, locked in on my purpose.

The battle is part of your growth; if you allow it, the struggle will strengthen you for challenges you have yet to face. Today, among other businesses, I own three daycare centers. I can't tell you how many children, families, and staff members have passed through our doors, but I know the impact has been greater than I could imagine! In that season, I learned that the fulfillment of my dream was close, but so was fear, and I had to learn to stand and do it afraid. Don't give up on your dreams!

Always remember growth takes time. Often, we want growth and the dream right now, but be patient; progress takes time. And to be honest, it's best to allow it to take its time. In 2015, I really considered closing everything down. I was exhausted from continuously hitting my head on the ceiling. I am positive that if it were not for lessons I learned in past battles and the circle of positive, influential people around me, I would have caved in and abandoned all. To throw in the towel then would have required starting all over later. Stay the course, and don't abandon your dreams; growth is happening even when you can't see it.

Continue to stay connected to your purpose. I believe this is one of the most important principles that I live by. I constantly roll the thought around in my head, "What is my purpose?" "Who am I here for?" "Who am I to impact?" That also keeps me connected to and constantly aware of my circle, my tribe, and my cheerleaders.

While in Paris, one of my biggest highlights was shopping in the Louis Vuitton boutique. There are levels in the shop, and when we were ready to go upstairs to the next level, we couldn't go alone. No one could go to the next level alone; everyone needed a guide. In obtaining your dreams, you cannot go to the next level alone; you need that team. You need people on your team who will help, encourage, and believe in you.

I've decided to live my life to the fullest — NOW. I don't want to put off the fun stuff, the growth, the opportunities to live life with family and friends, or to impact the world by snuffing out my dreams! I don't want to wait until I'm old or plan to simply leave a financial inheritance to my children that will allow them to achieve their dreams once I'm gone.

One evening before we left Paris, Steve and I sat on the balcony overlooking Paris, France, amazed by everything. You can do it too. DON'T GIVE UP ON YOUR DREAMS!

Delight yourself in the Lord and He will give you
the desires of your heart. ~ Psalm 37:4 (ESV)

Now It's Time To Invest

Think of a new experience you want to try. It doesn't have to be a trip to another country. It could be to dine at a restaurant you have wanted to try, learn a new language, go on a cruise, or parasail. Whatever it is, write it down.

What are your plans to make it happen?

What is one dream that keeps coming back no matter how you try to suppress it?

Your Purpose

The sooner you are authentically you, the sooner people looking for you will find you. ~ Myles Munroe

A lack of realism in the vision today costs credibility tomorrow. ~ John Maxwell

Don't let others tell you what you can't do. Don't let the limitations of others limit your vision. ~ Roy T. Benne

Don't settle for average. Bring your best to the moment. Then, whether it fails or succeeds, at least you know you gave all you had. ~ Angela Bassett

If you don't get out there and define yourself, you'll be quickly and inaccurately defined by others. ~ Michelle Obama

Old ways of doing things and closed minds will not attract growth. It's ok to evolve! #GrowOn ~ LaTonya Thorogood

The people who are crazy enough to think they can change the world are the ones who do. ~ Steve Jobs

When purpose is not known, abuse is inevitable ~ Myles Munroe

You cannot have a positive life and a negative mind. ~ Joyce Meyer

You'll never reach your destination if you stop and throw stones at every dog that barks. ~ Unknown

Leadership

Earn Team Buy In

Do you remember Toys R Us? I loved that store. Recently, we did a little research into why the company declared bankruptcy. This company, founded in 1957, laid off 33,000 employees in 2018. Why? What happened? Research findings seem to vary depending on where you look. However, the deterioration of the most crucial aspect of success was clear to me: there was a failure in leadership.

As I coach entrepreneurs concerning the need for team buy-in, we first discuss their leadership reputation. Through instruction and life lessons, I learned that people do not buy into a vision or idea until they trust the leader. The term *buy-in* refers to the members of your team understanding, accepting, and engaging in decisions and changes made within or affecting the organization. What does that mean? After all, you are the boss, CEO, and the one with authority to initiate change. Oh, it may be true that you are all that and more, but what you are not is capable of bringing about change in your company without team support, creativity, abilities, talents, and buy-in. You make the decision and are ultimately responsible for the results, but your team makes it happen, and that will not occur if you do not earn their respect.

Think about that for a moment. Buy-in doesn't begin in a boardroom or with a fantastic presentation. You cannot even earn it with a huge paycheck. You may purchase a person's service briefly, but their heart and earnest commitment are not for sale; these must be earned. Your idea, plan, product, or service may be everything I believe will succeed, but if your character and integrity as a leader are questionable, it's a wrap for me. I can tell you horror stories of times I've pushed past my gut sense that someone was flaky with questionable character and later wanted to put myself in a chokehold for ignoring the signs. Your staff must see that you, your leadership style, and your senior leadership team are worthy of their trust; then, you will find it less challenging to earn their buy-in.

Buy-in is vital to the organization because people will naturally work stronger when they believe in what they are doing. It builds team trust and helps create a more powerful team. Job satisfaction will increase when your staff feels connected and a part of the overall picture. With a sense of belonging, the individual members of your team will employ their talents more freely, releasing more creativity than either of you imagined.

Beyond checking and, if necessary, correcting your leadership reputation, how do you earn buy-in? While there are many ideas, I use four basic rules.

1. **SHARE THE VISION AND PLAN.** I talk to my senior leaders first and then the members of the teams to let them know about significant changes that will affect them. I understand that every idea will not cause an immediate celebration; change can be challenging. Where there is pushback, I remind myself it took me a moment to embrace the changes fully.

2. **ENCOURAGE CONVERSATION.** The established trust factor assures the team that they can ask questions and add their input. I listen with an open mind because I respect and value their opinion. I usually leave these sessions with worthwhile ideas and information.

3. **REMAIN CONNECTED.** Through follow-up and information-sharing sessions, I keep the team connected to the project and the progress. The maintained connection builds excitement and allows them to continue preparing. I remind myself that these team members have bought into the vision, and keeping their buy-in is vital to success.

4. **ADDRESS RESISTANCE.** Sometimes, when you introduce a new direction, there will be members of your team resistant to change. Open resistance can quickly turn to rebels and rouges infiltrating and infecting the rest of the team. I don't believe in "ignore the problem, and it will go away." My approach is to address this quickly with the individual to bring about a peaceful resolution for everyone concerned.

Once earned, team buy-in will reap the rewards and benefits you will need to maintain; it's not a one-time earn-and-forget event. The team's power is unity, which is strengthened by team buy-in. No matter how large or small your organization may be, never underestimate the power of buy-in or your need for its presence on your team.

Everything rises and falls on leadership. ~ John Maxwell

Now It's Time To Invest

Have you ever been part of an organization when significant changes occurred? How did leadership communicate the changes before and during the process?

How can the concept of earning team buy-in help in family relationships?

Brainstorm specific ways to handle resistance to a new idea or plan in your organization.

Are You a Productive Entrepreneur?

Let's go, girl; it's time to get up! We have a busy day before us! Rise and grind; no rest for the weary; it's time to be busy, busy, busy making moves; we have a timeline! You have to hustle to make it happen; don't waste time! Hop to it; let's get busy! And so, life goes, busy, busy, and busier. However, my question to you is, are you busy without productivity? Contrary to what it seems, busyness is not synonymous with getting things done.

Most people are busy. Just listen to conversations, and you will see I'm right. While you're evaluating the conversations of others, don't forget to listen to your own. I'm not attempting to change how we talk, but I want to challenge how we think about and approach productivity.

At the end of a long day, as you flop on the couch, have you ever thought, "What did I accomplish today?" Sometimes, I can tell you in general what I did: answered calls, responded to emails, and ran errands, but I can't put my finger on what I accomplished. Looking back, I realize in those days, I was swamped but not really productive. As successful entrepreneurs, our daily goal must be productivity over busyness.

We all have seven days a week. One day is for you to rest, and while most don't set aside a day a week to rest, for the sake of this example, we will assume that you do. If you submit to busyness for two of the remaining six days, potentially 1/3 of your time is nonproductive. At the end of the year, your busy days have cost you 104 days of productivity. Do you want tremendous success? I do. Then, let's tackle and flip the habit of busyness over productivity.

One of the great qualities missing from a busy day is discipline. Discipline keeps me on track and does not allow me to jump around doing a little bit of this, a little bit of that, and a whole lot of nothing. Self-discipline shields me from responding to internal and external distractions. It also gives me the internal support to stick to my priorities instead of allowing others to create them. Discipline prevents me from overstuffing my calendar and setting unrealistic expectations for myself. Expectations that will keep me busy and rob me of productivity.

One of the great tools I've found is planning. Self-discipline is easier when I invest a little time in the evening to plan and schedule for the following day. Don't schedule everything, but give your day structure and boundaries. I know someone who, on Sunday, looks at her schedule and the weather for the week and then prepares five outfits. She has disciplined herself, and unless a significant unexpected event occurs, she selects from those five outfits daily, saving herself time and frustration.

One of the key elements to gain control over in our quest to be more productive is distractions. There are so many attempts to pull at our attention and drain our time: social media, cell phone, email, notifications from every app we have, our wondering and wandering mind, family, pets, staff, a grumbling stomach, and on and on the list grows. To eliminate interruptions, turn off notifications on your phone. This will allow you to decide when to check-in. Schedule email checks in your day; typically, no email is so crucial that you must research and respond now. Schedule your focus time and set a timer. At the end of that time, grab something to eat, return phone calls, allow yourself time to do some of the busy work, and then return to focused productivity. There are many ways to eliminate distractions; find what works for you.

Evaluate your time usage. Track what you do, when you do it, and how much time you allow to do it. Eliminate the excess things that are not required and that you don't genuinely enjoy. For the necessary tasks that can be delegated to others, delegate them. Limit unlimited access to you. You should not answer every call and invest time in every caller when they call. That system allows many people to withdraw from your time account without permission. If you would not give them unlimited access to your bank account, don't give them unlimited access to your time account. Create boundaries, and don't feel you need to apologize for your life as a productive entrepreneur.

So, what do you think? Are you ready to reduce your busyness to increase productivity? No matter which calendar you look at — work, home, ministry, or personal — it's time to make the most of your time. It's the one resource you cannot get back.

Beware of the bareness of a busy life. ~ Socrates

Now It's Time To Invest

What are the biggest distractions in your life? What can you do to minimize or eliminate them?

Are there people in your life that you have given unlimited access to your time account that should not have that privilege? What is your plan to reduce their access without destroying the relationship?

List five things you can and are willing to do to become more productive and less busy.

The Conflict Manager

Everyone has a superpower, and some have several! You know that thing you do when you run into a room, spot the problem, and fix it. With all my hats, titles, and responsibilities, I must admit I have several superhero capes hanging in the closet. However, I've discovered that no matter what role I'm functioning in, there is one superpower I must use more than others. I am The Conflict Manager!

As a wife, mother, entrepreneur, teacher, lawyer, coach, pastor, or whatever your role is, you will find yourself in situations where conflict must be managed by someone other than those involved. Having the tools and skills in advance will serve you and others well.

There is nothing wrong with disagreeing; it's a normal part of every relationship. Disagreeing means I have a different opinion than you, and that's normal because I'm different from you in how and why I process things the way I do. The problem arises when the difference in opinion becomes emotionally charged by strong disagreement, clashing, and anger.

As The Conflict Manager, one of the first things we need to learn is managing conflict within ourselves. If you are a hothead prone to turn a difference of opinion into an all-out fussing match, your ability to diffuse other situations will be limited. As you try to calm the situation, others will think, "Really, you need a dose of your own medicine," and the value of your voice will decrease. As we discuss managing conflict in the following few paragraphs, remember to apply the principles and tips to yourself and others.

There are many ways to manage conflict; you must discover what works for you in the various areas of your world. There are plenty of resources on the market; invest time learning about this vital area. Let's look at a few basics that work well for me.

- **PREPARE THE TEAM IN ADVANCE.** Take time to teach conflict resolution to your groups, including your children. Preparing them in advance will help them manage the situation and provide others on the team with the tools to support conflict management, eliminating your need to get involved. I love it when my children work it out between themselves. My three children and our godson grew up in our home; they have their way of working through differences because they know the basics. In the businesses I own, my leadership teams and I are not called on much to resolve issues; through advanced training, the staff works through their process. Preparing the team in advance creates winning opportunities for everyone.

- **TEACH PERSONAL RESPONSIBILITY.** Set an example and teach others to step back or walk away when the situation escalates. Often, those in conflict need to be correct and convince others they are right. Teach them the value of having the courage and self-confidence to walk away, not in anger or defeat but in victory. There is great value in knowing when to speak and when to be silent. Walking away allows both to work through feelings, so when the conversation is revisited, there is a greater chance of resolving the situation.

- **WATCH YOUR WORDS.** Words are powerful; they bring peace or war. Teach your team to use their words wisely. Avoid the horrible words *never, always, every,* and *all* in a disagreement. Refrain from attacking and finger-pointing. Watch the tone and volume of your voice. I've heard that 10% of conflict is differing opinions, and 90% is tone and delivery. The right thing said with the wrong tone or volume will not bring resolution to the situation. Teaching others to express their perspective and feelings peacefully, positively, and non-confrontational is priceless.

- **USE YOUR EARS.** Listen. When the other person speaks, open your ears and your heart. Teach your team to avoid listening to respond; instead, listen to understand. Even if you disagree, understanding the other person's position will give you great insight and sometimes allow a compromise to resolve the situation.

- **AVOID HOLDING A GRUDGE.** Learning to let it go is essential. When a situation is resolved, holding on to resentment is like holding on to hot coal; it only hurts you and the team. One of the most important members of any team is the peacemaker. They are the ones who will return to ensure everything is all right and everyone is genuinely moving forward without grudges.

Sometimes, we must agree to disagree when conflict arises but still work in unity and peace. Show me an atmosphere, family, or business charged with conflict and people at odds with each other, and I will show you a team that is not living up to its full potential and a less-than-successful organization. Division destroys. Look at Matthew 12:25, "Any kingdom that fights against itself is reduced to ruins. And any family or community splintered by strife will fall apart."

Every group and team occasionally need assistance to manage conflict, so I'm deputizing you as The Conflict Manager in your world. Now, it's up to you to train yourself and other leaders in your organization to manage, not ignore, when conflict arises. The health of your team depends on it.

If we only listened with the same passion that we
feel about being heard. ~ Harriet Lerner

Now It's Time To Invest

What can you gain from walking away from a conflict? Is it difficult for you to put a conversation on hold until a better time?

Think of the last time you were involved in resolving conflict; what could you have done differently to diffuse the situation?

How do you determine when it's time to speak and when it's time to be silent?

Intimidated by My Own Thoughts of Success

Thirty years ago, when I opened my first in-home daycare beyond high school, I only had a few hours from a community college under my belt, but I had a vision and a dream that burned within me. As the years passed, I continued faithfully in the arena I felt was my life assignment, taking classes and attending training to assist me in perfecting my craft. In the meantime, my husband, who had a bachelor's degree in accounting when we got married, was earning his bachelor's in Christian Education and pursuing his master's in accounting. I can't tell you how often people questioned my lack of what they considered "formal" education.

My own thoughts of success attempted to intimidate me as I considered my lack of traditional education. My portfolio just didn't seem to stack up as it was compared to others. The questioning looks hit their mark, and ultimately, deep down inside, I began to question myself.

My intimidation was hidden from many, even some closest to me. I was good at covering up the intimidation with determination. I was determined to grab that ring of success to silence the loud voices that doubted me because of the lack they saw. I walked confidently, worked with determination, and continued pushing forward. I took classes and sought opportunities to enter programs that helped me to excel in my ambitions. I began to experience and even enjoy success in my business, yet with every great goal, I continued to battle the intimidation of my thoughts of success.

At some point, I decided enough, no more. I decided to succeed in this area and be done with this battle. Today, I stand still without a diploma from a "traditional" institute of higher learning, but I am no longer intimidated by my thoughts or the thoughts of others. I am a champion, and everything I place my heart, mind, and hands to succeeds! God has positioned me to stand in the presence of great men and women to teach and be taught. I'm not arrogant, but I'm confident that I was born to achieve greatness while teaching others there is more than one way to succeed. The thoughts that came to intimidate me are now the stools I use to reach heights I never considered possible. Those who fed my negative thoughts with their negative words and opinions are welcomed in my coaching program as they also deserve to be freed from daunting thoughts that keep them from their own success.

How did you get there, Coach? The road map is simple.

- **SELF-ACCEPTANCE.** I'm so proud of my husband, children, and others who have obtained their associate's, bachelor's, master's, or doctorate degrees. However, I am equally proud of the formal and informal education I have received. I have learned there is no single road to success, no cookie-cutter way to make it; there are many ways. The most important thing is to determine your path. Accept and respect you and your road to success.

- **BE INSPIRED.** Don't be intimidated by others; be inspired! See others as teachers, not as competition. I am only in competition with my yesterday self. When my husband and I accepted the call to pastor, my old enemy of intimidation tried to raise its head again. Steve has a master's degree in Christian Education. He has studied scriptures I haven't even read. I could see and understand him as a Pastor, but me? And yet, here I am, not intimidated but secure in what God has called me to do. Secure that, as always, He has ensured everything I need to accomplish all He assigned to my life has already been made available to me. I have stood beside great men and women, humbled by our encounter but not intimidated.

- **SUCCESSFUL PEOPLE ARE FLAWED.** Don't put people on a pedestal; no one is as perfect as you think. No matter how wealthy, educated, influential, talented, or famous a person is, they still have flaws. When people put others on an elevated platform, they tend to forget humanness, the flaws, and the areas that are just not right. You should never measure yourself against anyone; when you attempt to compare yourself to someone you have lifted up, you will always come up short.

Be careful about looking at yourself through a magnifying glass and others through rose-colored glasses.

- **THERE IS ALWAYS ROOM AT THE TOP.** As a coach, I know I am NOT the coach for everyone. As the owner of three child development and learning centers, I know our centers are not the perfect place for every child. I understand there is room in the circle of success for more than a few businesses. There is no reason to be intimidated because someone else in your area is offering the same services as your business; there is room at the top for everyone who wants to succeed. Celebrate with others as they achieve victories, and watch them do the same for you!

Don't allow intimidating thoughts to shut out thoughts of success! Go for it; you were created to succeed!

Life has no limitations except the
ones we make. ~ Les Brown

Now It's Time To Invest

Are you intimidated by the successes of others as you compare them to your accomplishments? What is one thing you are willing to do to overcome that intimidation?

What is the difference between confident and cocky, arrogant and self-assured?

Have you given someone in your life permission to check you when you cross the line of being cocky or intimidated? (Neither is beneficial to your success.) If so, call and ask them where you stand. If not, identify one and permit them to watch out for your blindside.

Boss Move

Every year, my big, wonderful family gets together, and we invade Myrtle Beach! It's always an incredible time filled with everything a family vacation should contain. I'll tell you the truth; I don't even like the beach. Sinking my feet in the sand does not appeal to me at all. However, every year, I look forward to it because it's so much bigger than the beach; it's about the family, and the memories are priceless.

While I can swim, you can imagine the idea of water play at the beach is something I can live without. I usually let the family go, and I stay back, cleaning and preparing for our next group excursion. However, in 2018, I took a giant leap; I got on my first jet ski. Ok, let me not paint a picture of an athlete attacking the waves. When I say I got on, I mean I got on with my oldest daughter, Nikki, who of my children is the safest and least aggressive jet skier. We ride at a pace that doesn't take my breath away but gives me that jet ski experience. On the other hand, my other children are zooming around, riding the waves, and breaking the speed limits set in my mind of what's safe! That one giant leap to do something I had never done before propelled me from the shores of the known into the unknown and the amazingly beautiful. I had never seen the ocean from this perspective; it's a different kind of beautiful.

What I did in 2018 — mounting that jet ski — is an example of a *Boss Move*. The term boss move is typically attributed to something an athlete does on the court or field that screams, "I am the ONE!" without saying a single word. It shows who is in charge at that moment. As the mom of a professional basketball player, I know from experience that when a boss move is made, everyone on your team and in your corner goes wild! That single silent move pumps fire into the place, and the atmosphere shifts.

A boss move is a purposeful strategy or course of action that takes you out of your comfort zone to achieve something extraordinary. In business, boss moves are defining moments where entrepreneurs make decisions with the ultimate goal of being projected forward on their path to success and the next level. I love making boss moves, especially when they work. Yes, you heard me when they work. I know you have learned, just as I have, that plans don't always go as you envisioned.

I recall once I tried to help a fellow entrepreneur from a local city save her business. She had a children's playhouse, something like Chuck E. Cheese. I put my finances into the commitment before researching and processing the application through the state licensing agency. We started watching children, and I hired a small staff. During the licensing process, I discovered it would cost more than I was willing and prepared to invest in keeping the business open. We had to close the doors.

While that didn't work as planned, it still had value. I learned I did not fail. I am always about learning, but I am not, have never been, and will never be a failure. Just as I don't have time to boast about my successes, I don't have time to wallow in my misses. I take what I can learn and move forward.

As a successful entrepreneur, you must be willing to do the things you have never done. Extraordinary achievements will not come to the person determined to do the same thing the same way. Like Albert Einstein said, *"Insanity is doing the same thing over and over and expecting different results."* In the times when the results are not what you anticipated, learn and keep moving forward. Do not allow yourself or anyone else to attach the label of failure to you or your dreams.

I love how my family and friends celebrate when I'm successful. However, I absolutely appreciate the way they keep the pom-poms in their hands when my attempts prove less than profitable. I couldn't live a double life with one group of people to celebrate the wins and another to encourage the tough lessons.

In 2013, my company went through a significant financial struggle. I almost lost the business. The owners threatened that I would have to move if I didn't come up with $20,000 by the end of October 2013. Supportive family and friends rallied beside me. Many of them donated finances that allowed my business to continue. Less than four months later, in February 2014, I was offered the opportunity to open another school. Considering that

I almost lost everything just a few months earlier, it didn't make sense to consider opening another school. I've learned that boss moves don't always make sense. I prayed for God's guidance, knowing that if He said "go", everything I needed was already waiting for me. In 2014, I opened my second center, Pam's Place, in honor of my mother, who passed away in April 2014 from cancer.

A song I love says, *"Fear is not my future, You are."* As an entrepreneur, the day you allow fear to take the driver's seat, you stop succeeding, and your dreams will begin to fade. Did you make some wrong moves? Me too. You moved forward when you should have stood still? Me too. You lost some people you should have held onto? Me too. You held on to some people you should have released? Me too. You stopped dreaming and are sitting stagnant, afraid to move forward? NOT ME! I'm about to make a boss move forward. Come on, join me!

> *It's time for you to move, realizing that the thing you are seeking is also seeking you.* ~ Iyanla Vanzant

Now It's Time To Invest

Is there a BOSS MOVE stirring on the inside of you? This blank sheet of paper is a judgment-free zone. Use this space to brainstorm. Include what you perceive to be your hurdles and roadblocks, internal and external.

CEO — Conquer Every Obstacle

For years, I dreamed, prayed, prepared, and planned. I looked at potential properties, met with realtors, and flirted with the possibilities of various locations. I attended courses and began shifting the systems within my in-home daycare to match my vision for the child development center I would own. In 2006, it happened! All negotiations were complete, contracts signed, and I was standing in the middle of *Nikki's Christian Daycare Center*; I was the owner and CEO!

In the middle of that dream-come-true moment, in my sweet innocence to the business world, I could not understand the weight of those three letters. However, I quickly learned that as **C**hief **E**xecutive **O**fficer, if I desired to thrive, I needed to learn to **C**onquer **E**very **O**bstacle.

As an entrepreneur, you will face many, did I say many, obstacles. Enjoy the minor ones because there will be others that will threaten to take your breath away. I'm not trying to discourage you; I desire to prepare you. Here is the good news: you have the potential to overcome every challenging situation you face. I want you to think about that and say it aloud to yourself. Repeat it without hesitation or the question mark in your voice. It is true, and the best time to believe that is before the obstacles appear.

Obstacles are not limited to entrepreneurs; everyone will face barriers that seem to stand in the way of where you are and your destination: limited revenue, family situations, time constraints, employee struggles, management issues, and health problems. The possibilities are endless. However, I have discovered that the most significant obstacle with the ultimate potential to end your dreams and destroy your vision is your decision not to conquer the challenges you face. I promise you the hurdle will not go away if you do nothing. Failure to respond will allow the situation to grow and impact other areas of your life.

"Ok, Coach Nikki, what do I do?" Glad you asked; let's look at a 4-point plan I believe you can use to approach and conquer every obstacle.

1. **DO NOT ALLOW FEAR TO TAKE THE DRIVER'S SEAT.** I don't want to say, "Don't be afraid," because there are situations where fear will come; it's what you do with the fear, the power you grant the fear that is the key. Fear is an emotion, a natural response to a challenging situation. However, fear is not the street I live on. Fear, if allowed to rule, will choke and paralyze. The way to overcome the obstacle will be hindered if your mind and heart are wrapped up in fear. You must choose to invest your energy in discovering a solution to immobilize

the obstacle versus pondering the possibilities of what will happen if the challenge before you wins.

2. **GATHER THE TEAM.** If you sit with me for more than 10 minutes, you will always hear me talk about my team in one way or another. To become and remain successful, you must have a team of trusted individuals with various skill sets, gifts, and talents. Team members that you can be transparent with during the challenges. Yes, people who will gather to encourage you, but they will also lend themselves and their resources to see you past the challenge that towers in your path.

3. **DO THE RESEARCH.** As a team, brainstorm possible solutions and initiate the research process. Sometimes, the answer is a combination of several ideas, something you would have never thought of alone. Researching will open options you never knew existed. Programs, organizations, and support systems exist for almost everything; my friend Google taught me that. As a team, accept the challenge of finding a way to bring down the barricade.

4. **ACT.** I've seen people overpowered by a challenge because they remain stuck in research mode. They were so concerned with "what if it doesn't work" they never tried anything. Do you recall what I said earlier? *"Failure to respond will allow the situation to grow and impact other areas of your life."* You must do something. What if you make the wrong decision? Ok, stop and go back with your team and form another plan. You didn't fail; you just learned what didn't work. Get up and continue moving forward.

Say it again: *"I have the potential to overcome every challenging and difficult situation that I face."* Believe it and believe in yourself. You have this!

> *There will be obstacles. There will be doubters.*
> *There will be mistakes. But with hard work,*
> *there are no limits.* ~ Unknown

Now It's Time To Invest

Is there an obstacle between you and the success of your dreams? Identify it. What team members will you gather? By what date will you contact them?

How have you responded to obstacles in the past?

Is transparency in struggles a problem for you? In writing, dialogue your answer with yourself.

Why do you believe that you have the potential to overcome every challenging and difficult situation you face?

Give Yourself Permission to Fail

Have you ever allowed thoughts of past blunders to create a concrete ceiling above your head that prevented you from seeing, much less reaching higher heights? It's like a barrier that causes you to settle for what you have because, clearly, in your thinking, it's all you will obtain. After all, remember the past. I did. Man, I have fought thoughts that I would never get beyond where I was at that moment because of all my business mistakes.

How did I get off the cycle of dream-killing doom? First, it was by the grace of God and the prayers of my Mom, Dad, husband, family, and friends. I had no choice but to pick myself up and keep moving forward. Second, I had to learn to permit myself to fail.

I know the second one seems a little counterproductive, but stick with me for a bit longer, and I promise it will make sense. You see, I had to learn that failure happens, but it is never meant to be the moment that defines me. I came to realize no one said, "Nicole. You are a failure!" I put that pressure on myself.

Next, I had to learn to use what others might have classified as a failure to my advantage. What others would have embraced as a blunder, I began investigating as an opportunity. Did you know that Walt Disney was fired from a local Kansas City newspaper because he lacked creativity? Rowland Hussey experienced seven business failures before he founded Macy's. Did you hear about the young evening news reporter who was fired? The producer said she was unfit for television; now you get to watch her show, and you get to watch her show, and you get to watch her show! Everyone gets to watch her show! Way to go, Ms. Oprah Winfrey. What was the difference between their failure and those who afterward took their dream to the grave? I had to find out because I would not be the latter!

As you give yourself permission to fail, keep your great value in mind; nothing as valuable as you can be a failure. You just learned what didn't work for you. You discovered that person didn't belong in your life; after all, everyone isn't for you. Learn to face your past missteps quickly; don't allow them to become towering giants. Never let past failures paralyze you; fear has no place in your future. Just get up, dust off, and keep it moving forward. That moment you failed will become a couple of pages in your story, not the whole book, and certainly not the end!

Success looks absolutely gorgeous on me, and it looks great on you, too! I celebrate that I did not give up; I celebrate me! Do you celebrate yourself?

You better!!! In fact, I want to thank myself for not quitting even when I failed. I want to thank me for loving me and trusting God. I want to say, "Thank you, Nicole, for accepting every pitfall and allowing it to turn you into a better you. YOU ROCK GIRL!!!"

My celebration is over; now let's celebrate you! Get up, embrace the grace, and move forward. Give yourself permission to fail.

Anytime you feel overwhelmed or unsure, remember your why. Why did you start? Why is this your passion? ~ Stephanie Brown, Daughter

Now It's Time To Invest

Often, you are the toughest on yourself. Where do you need to ask yourself for forgiveness? Do it right here. No one is looking. I know it seems a little crazy, but if you had treated and talked to someone else like you did to yourself, they would have left you. Go ahead and apologize.

Take what you once considered a failure and dissect it. Look for the opportunity to use it to your advantage. What happened? What can you learn for the next time? Remember, don't shift the blame; own it. Only when you have the remote control can you change the channel.

Celebrate the Wins

The Brown's home is always filled with celebrations. Holidays, birthdays, big gameday, departures, arrivals, weddings, business launches, and more, we celebrate around here. I love the festive mood with laughter bouncing off the walls, great food, and people everywhere enjoying themselves. While celebrating big accomplishments is always a hit, there are occasions that could be easily overlooked that warrant remembering as well; we call those the "small" wins.

Grand visions are made up of many small wins accomplished by a team that helps you translate your dreams into action. Celebrating those small wins encourages and motivates team members between the start and finish line. In my business, family, friends, business associates, staff, and life, I look for opportunities to celebrate small wins of the team, individuals, and myself. I don't wait until the major victories are won or the final goals are obtained.

Let's define the term "small wins." I don't want you to think they are wins with less value; without the small wins, the ultimate goal or win would never happen. Small wins are the accomplishments made in pursuit of a primary objective. For example, if your goal is to lose 50 pounds, when you lose 5 or 10 pounds, it's celebration time. If a company aims to increase production by 100 widgets at 25 widgets, it's time to rally the team, acknowledging that we are moving forward. Let me share some of the reasons I live by this approach.

Celebrating the team's victories along the journey is a way to strengthen the sense of connection and strong work culture. When you take time to acknowledge and applaud the small wins of a team, it motivates the crew and encourages them to strive for greater success. Sporadic celebrations boost morale and build loyalty as it energizes the group, reminding them they are a part of something tremendous and that each piece is vital.

When you make it a habit of celebrating the small wins of your team members, you boost their confidence and increase their desire to invest their gift into the objective. You also allow others to see that hard work pays off and is appreciated. Members of your team who feel valued and celebrated will become more dedicated to your organization's vision. Not only will you improve their self-confidence, but you will also boost the reputation of your business and improve the retention of good performers.

How do you celebrate? Anyway, you want to. Walk through the building with a bullhorn announcing the achievements and reward with an extra 30 minutes for lunch. Buy lunch or a coffee doughnut combination for the achievers. If it's the team you're recognizing, order lunch, play music, and dance a victory dance. You are only limited by your own imagination; it's not what you do but the fact that you do something to acknowledge the accomplishment.

Don't forget to celebrate yourself with your team, family, and friends. It's important that they celebrate your small wins with you; it's another way to build the crew's unity and gives everyone a visual reminder that celebrating the small wins is vital.

So, grab some confetti, and let's start this party; we have reasons to celebrate.

> *Small wins are still won, and the journey is more important than overnight success.* ~ Bill Watterson

Now It's Time To Invest

Brainstorm ways you can celebrate small wins for the following people. Use your imagination more than your money, and invest your time.

- *Spouse*
- *Parents*
- *Children*
- *Staff workers*
- *Business Partner*
- *Yourself*

Select three from above and carry out your idea—Journal about your activity and the recipient's reaction.

To help keep the idea alive, sporadically enter small win celebrations for the year on your calendar. It will remind you to look for opportunities to celebrate until it becomes second nature for you.

Where Are We Growing To?

In my family, business endeavors, and plans for personal development, I continually ask myself, *"Where are we growing to?"* Then, I take the time to think about the question and respond to myself. Yes, I do talk to myself and admit it, and so do you. In fact, I talk to myself more than anyone else, so I find my conversations with me tend to have the most significant influence and impact on my direction and courses of action.

My carefully thought-out answers are like road signs on a long trip; they assure me that I'm still on the correct route or warn me that I'm off course. In these reflective moments, I can evaluate if my resources are being used most effectively or if I need to shift. I assess my own input and investment into the endeavor. Have I stepped back too far, or am I too close, hindering the creativity of others on the team? During this time, I'm honest with myself, holding no punches because I know sustained growth will only occur at the rate that I can lead.

Once I have the answers to my question, *"Where are we growing to?"* I gather the team to share my discoveries. The team must be aware of our direction.

If we have holes or weaknesses in the plan, I assume responsibility as the leader, and together, we discuss how to strengthen the team and get back on track. We are a team, all wearing the same color jersey, although we wear different numbers and assume different roles. We are collectively working together to achieve the same goal. We celebrate together if we are on track; it's everyone's victory party. Everyone on my team knows victory for one is a victory for all; the rewards of success are enjoyed by everyone, just as each person shares the responsibility to produce.

When was the last time you really took a break to discover where you are growing to in your family, businesses, health, finances, and personal development? I know you started out with a plan, but if you have not given your plan a checkup, it could be outdated, or you may have already obtained your goals and are currently functioning just to operate without a target to aim toward. I encourage you to invest this week to stop and go through the process of asking and answering the question, *"Where are we growing to?"* Then do something with the answers you discover! It's time for a checkup!

> *You don't drown by falling in the water; you*
> *drown by staying there.* ~ Edwin Louis Cole

Now It's Time To Invest

Select three areas in your life and go through the process of determining "Where are we growing to?" Don't feel guilty about the areas you do not choose, and don't overload yourself by attempting to evaluate all areas. This week, select one of the three areas daily and assess the growth.

Schedule a meeting with those on your team in the area you evaluated. Share your discoveries, celebrate the victories, and create plans to course correct where needed.

After seeing your progress with the one area you selected, I hope you'll also take the time beyond this week to work on growing in the other two areas.

Thrive with Your Tribe

I am one of the wealthiest women in the world! Oh, you doubt me? Well, your opinion will never change my perspective; I am undoubtedly one of the wealthiest women in the world. The question you should ask is how I define wealth. You see, my definition of wealth is centered on the people I have in my life. Sometimes, I call them my tribe, and other times, my circle. They are also known as my family, friends, cheerleaders, and sisters. Regardless of how I refer to them, they are the people who are there for me.

I cannot imagine my life without the people surrounding me, supporting, encouraging, correcting, and standing with me. There have been changes over the years; some have gone, and others have come. But consistently, I have been surrounded by people who add tremendous value to me, my life, my family, and my businesses. The value of those who left has not diminished; many left an unerasable mark of greatness that I will never forget, and all left me with lessons for life.

What does your tribe look like? Mine are just as diverse, inside and outside, as the stars in the sky. I believe it is the diversity that makes us mighty. In areas where I am not strong, a member of my tribe has me covered, and in the areas where I have strength, I cover them. Just as there's no comparing the beauty of each sunset, there's no comparing the value of each member of my circle. No comparison and no competition.

How do you connect with the members of your circle? Connection is vital to creating lasting and trusting relationships. People in my circle or tribe have access to me that casual acquaintances do not have, and rightly so. Just as they have access to me, I have access to them. To connect, you must invest your time and heart.

Does your tribe believe in and support you, even when they don't understand where you are going? Some sisters in my circle do not own a business, and while they do not understand my decisions, I find their support and input invaluable.

Are your circles filled with only family members? I know my family loves me, and they follow me, cheering me on to success. However, I find a level of support outside of my family. It doesn't negate the value of my family; it simply speaks to my need for more in my tribal circles.

How do you celebrate your tribe? I have discovered that every celebration is not the same. You must decide what works for you and your crew. Be creative and look for ways to celebrate the members of your tribe, opportunities to say thank you, and acknowledge the value they add to your life. A phone call, a lunch date, a thank you note, or a special gift; the possibilities are endless.

As well as them supporting you, don't forget to encourage them in their endeavors. Think about how much it blesses you when they stand up for you. Supporting, encouraging, and showing up for my tribe is natural for me; it blesses me as much as it blesses them. I keep my high school cheerleading pom poms and cheerleading moves ready. No matter where they are in the world, they know I am here!

My tribe and circles of support are one of the reasons I thrive in my endeavors! I can't imagine life or success without them. The paths I walk are wide; they must be in order to accommodate all the people given to me to complete my life assignments. I seldom walk alone.

In *The 21 Irrefutable Laws of Leadership*, John Maxwell states, *"One is too small a number to achieve greatness."* Don't attempt to accomplish anything great alone; connect to your tribe.

> *Success is empty if you arrive at the finish*
> *line alone. The best reward is to get there*
> *surrounded by winners.* ~ Howard Schultz

Now It's Time To Invest

Who are the main people in your tribe?

How do you celebrate them?

Take a moment to send the people you listed a note to let them know how much you value their presence in your life.

Who is no longer in your circle, but their impact on your life is unerasable? Write them a note and let them know their investment is still bringing returns.

Delegate and Let Go!

As leaders, entrepreneurs, women, mothers, grandmothers, wives, corporate executives, or whatever title we hold, we have all said more than once, "I NEED HELP!" There is so much to do and so little time to accomplish everything. After all, our superhero power is not growing 14 other arms in the blink of an eye; extra arms that will do everything on our list! Looking back, I see no matter how many people raised their hand to answer my 911 call for assistance, the help they provided always seemed to fall short of the help I needed.

In 2017, after about 25 years as an entrepreneur, I realized the problem wasn't the people sent to help; the problem was me. That was the year I learned that you cannot keep complaining about needing help if you refuse to allow the HELP TO HELP! That year, I realized I needed to let my directors do their jobs without me hovering over them; I needed to stop assigning my assistant tasks while I stayed up at night researching what I expected her to discover. Not only was I duplicating efforts and wasting resources of time, money, and energy, but I was also attacking the confidence and crippling the growth potential of those around me. I was stifling my leadership team, and in that, I was hindering the company's growth, family, relationships, and businesses.

Why do we put people in leadership positions but never allow them to lead? We have trained them, provided examples of how to do the job or task, sent them to 5,000 training seminars, mentored them, and invested in them with our hearts and soul. At some point, we must delegate and let it go. We must allow them to show us what they learned in the process. Prepare yourself as you delegate and let go; others will make mistakes, but so did you. No one will do it exactly like you, but that is alright. There is more than one way to arrive at a destination successfully.

After my great awakening, I felt it was time to have my own office to focus on the business. Making that significant change gave me more clarity and freedom as a business owner. The move opened the door for me to do what I had heard at every conference; I began to work on the business, not in the business. I will not tell you it was a smooth and straightforward transition; it was a process, but my resolve was strengthened as I witnessed something extraordinary. During the process, I saw my well-trained and prepared staff step up and grow what was blooming inside of them.

How many of you have people you have assigned to leadership positions right now but have never allowed them to lead? Truthfully ask and answer yourself the following questions.

- Have you built your team?
- Have you trained your team?
- Do you challenge your team?
- Do you trust your team?
- Do you listen to your team?
- Do you invest in your team?
- Do you check in with your team?
- Do you individually and collectively thank your team?

If you can truthfully answer yes that you consistently do those things, it's time to delegate and let go. If your answers are no, it's time to invest in and prepare your team to receive the responsibility and authority as you position them and yourself for the future.

One of my wisest decisions for my businesses, staff, family, and myself was to learn to delegate and let go! Trust me, you will never go back.

If you want to do a few small things right, do them yourself. If you want to do great things and make a big impact, learn to delegate. ~ John Maxwell

Now It's Time To Invest

Think back to the last time you assigned someone a task, and you went back, openly, or privately, to "help," "perform an in-progress evaluation," or "alter the direction of the project" because it was not as you would have done it. Were your actions necessary? Looking back, is it possible the result would have been a success without your intervention?

Do you believe there is another way to accomplish an assignment, or is your way the only road to success?

Do you micromanage? Ask others who work with you and family members to answer that question: Do you micromanage? Are the answers the same? Now, you choose what to do with the information you discover.

Don't Get Chained to the Comments

There is no getting around it; social media is here to stay, and its presence is a powerful influence in our world. I admit I'm one of the connected ones, and as an entrepreneur with businesses in several fields, I have a few accounts. Although I have a team to manage my social media presence, I spend time on the accounts as I monitor our overall marketing strategy.

I share that to say social media is not a villain; it's not bad. In fact, as a coach to entrepreneurs, one of the areas I work on with clients is their social media presence, and I have someone who works with me on mine. A great marketing plan includes maximizing your use of social platforms. Social media reduces your marketing expenses, makes you and your business more visible, and provides a place for you and your customers to have a voice. The use of social media is critical for all entrepreneurs as it allows a limitless audience to build excitement and hype for new and existing products and services. My concern is not the product; it's the obsession with it.

Humor me for a moment and take a quick quiz. Answer the following questions honestly.

- Do you constantly check your social media accounts? Are you connected first thing in the morning, throughout the day, last thing in the evening, while on a date, when talking to others on the phone, while in meetings, at the movies, and so on?
- When you are focused on doing something else, do you allow interruptions as your thoughts drift to what's happening on social media? Mental intrusions that cause you to stop and look?
- Do you invest the time to read all the comments?
- After reading the comments, do you repeat them, mentally or verbally, good and bad?
- Do you invest time attempting to validate the legitimacy of negative commenters by trolling their pages?

With your yes answers, think about how much time you invest unnecessarily in social media as you stray from the real purpose and value into being preoccupied with the comments and the emoji interactions. I want to encourage you not to get shackled to the comments.

Working with clients, I researched and discovered that social media meets a natural human need to be recognized, respected, and appreciated. A need that real people in our life should meet is fed by "friends" we never met. This new way of feeding the need is training our brains to respond to the "loves" and "likes" much as we react to a hug from someone we love. Our emotional needs are being paid for with eHugs from strangers.

The problem occurs when the eHug turns into an eSlap. Social media is filled with "social media warriors," who will say whatever comes to mind. People who drop nuggets of foolishness and sit back to watch the reactions. Wise men speak because they have something to say; social media warriors speak because they have an audience and a platform. Without concern for others, safe behind their screen, just because they can, they sling mindless words.

While you can't control those warriors, you can control the warrior within yourself. Don't allow yourself to get chained to the comments. Be confident in yourself, your business, and your ideas. Don't allow unknown, uninformed, and uninvested strangers to change your course of action. Stand firm and confident. If you have thin skin and are easily offended, social media and the business world will rip at your heart and send you into a tailspin, injecting confusion and doubt into your vision. You must "toughen up buttercup."

Do not overvalue what you read or hear. Just as you would not take medical advice from an unskilled, unknown, self-proclaimed expert, don't waste your valuable time with others whose negative input should have no attacking power. Learn to separate foolishness from comments that warrant a closer look. Use all your marketing platforms for their intended purpose to grow and promote your business, but don't get chained to the comments, and don't allow them to change your heart, passion, or direction.

You have this! Be the boss on social media, but don't let social media boss you.

> *Social media gives legions of idiots the right to speak when they once only spoke at a bar after a glass of wine, without harming the community, but now they have the same right to speak as a Nobel Prize winner.* ~ Umberto Eco

Now It's Time To Invest

Brainstorm some ways to allow social media to become a more effective tool for you and less of a deficiency.

Open a conversation with other business owners in your circle concerning being cuffed to the comments. There is wisdom and strength in your circle of supporters.

Monitor your time on social media; are you spending your greatest resource wisely? If not, how do you change your poor investment choices?

Building the Business Team

In 2005, while attending a course at the Women's Business Center in Virginia, I really learned one of my most valuable business lessons. I say, "I really learned" because I've known and used the principle before, but that evening, it exploded like never before, forever changing me as a businesswoman and leader.

> In business, you often look for and capitalize on your strengths, but when you are earnestly ready to grow your organization, identify and make provisions for your weaknesses. You accomplish that by looking for someone whose strength is your weakness.

I later realized that tidbit of wise information is one of the primary lessons in building a rock-solid, effective business team. An effective team promotes creativity and takes advantage of different strengths and experiences. Working as a group, the well-built team can produce results beyond what any individual member could do alone. It's a team that will excel at every challenge because they have learned to respect and use each other's strengths. A strong team, however, will not build or maintain itself; that is the responsibility of leadership.

Here are a few essential tips to go in your leadership toolbox.

- **INVEST TIME.** Invest time in getting to know your team members and allow them to get to know you. When you spend time together, you will also learn their strengths and weaknesses, assisting them in professional and personal development. You will get the best from your team when they see that you care about them. Theodore Roosevelt said, *"People don't care how much you know until they know how much you care."*
- **COMMUNICATE...COMMUNICATE.** Ensure you share information promptly and equitably. Your senior leadership team should hear the news together. When you share with various people at different times, you cause confusion and ill feelings. Share the information concisely and avoid vague explanations that leave more questions than they answer.
- **INSPECT THE APPLES.** Do not allow renegades to destroy your team's unity or keep the team from succeeding. Also, do not allow those producing below the acceptable level to stand with those working with heart and soul. One bad apple will spoil the whole bunch if given the opportunity.
- **RESPECT EVERYONE AND THEIR TALENT.** One of the most important things a leader can do is to stand back and let talented people work. When you're constantly hovering over their shoulder, you're essentially saying that you don't trust them to do their job. Have faith in your team!

- **SAY THANK YOU.** One great thing you can do is to show your team how much you appreciate their efforts. Whether you take them out to lunch or something as simple as letting them leave a little early, rewarding your team can go a long way toward building and maintaining a fabulous business team.

Above all, as you are building your business team, consider how you would want to be treated. In your attempts to strive for greatness, never forget that the most excellent leader is the one who remembers the value of the team.

Hire people who are better than you are, then
leave them to get on with it. ~ David Ogilvy

Now It's Time To Invest

Consider three of the most common obstacles to building a rock-solid, effective business team: vague goals, lack of trust, and ineffective communication. Brainstorm below how to overcome these obstacles. If you want to step your brainstorming session up a notch, invite a few business associates or team members to join you.

1. Vague goals.

2. Lack of trust.

3. Ineffective communication.

Leadership

You grow at your level of exposure.
~ Stephen L. Brown, Husband

The more people you help become successful, the more successful you become. ~ Steve Harvey

Leadership is a visual thing. ~ John Maxwell

Before you can inspire your players to win, you have to show them how not to lose. ~ Bob Knight

No risk is without some type of stretch in you. ~ Carol Jones, Friend

When you delegate tasks, you create followers. When you delegate authority, you create leaders. ~ Craig Groeschel

I want "go-getters," not people I have to go get. ~ Sabrina Sanchez, Friend

If your actions inspire others to dream more, learn more, do more, and become more, you are a leader. ~ Simon Sinek

Business Partner? Are You Sure?

Before Steve and I got married, our pastor at the time required extensive pre-marital counseling before he would perform the ceremony. We soon realized he knew some things our youthful exuberance had not taught us. Much of what he shared and had us think about, we had never considered. We were in love and ready to start our life together. Like many others, we figured we would work through our troubles as they happened. What could go wrong? After all, as I said, we were in love. On the other side of "I do," we were happy we submitted to the preparation. While nothing could prepare us for every challenge and hurdle we encountered, the counseling helped us to avoid many pitfalls.

While business partnerships are common among entrepreneurs and solve many start-ups' financial concerns, they come with potential relationship-severing, business-destroying problems. In many ways, deciding to enter business with another person is comparable to entering into a marriage.

Unlike investors who invest their finances and only expect the promised return on their investment, a partner is responsible and involved in the business. This intimate involvement can cause significant conflicts, including the company's collapse.

There are just as many reasons for friction in a partnership as the stars in the sky. For example, breakdown in trust, different priorities, the disparity in time or financial investment, management style, power or role imbalances, values, personality clashes, staffing approach differences, or the color of the carpet.

An old saying is, "An ounce of prevention is worth a pound of cure." Here are a few partnership troubles and a few thoughts on how to avoid them.

- **INEQUITABLE DEDICATION.** Before entering a partnership, determine if the prospective partner is equally committed to the endeavor. Not only will it be a challenge to keep the business thriving if you and your business partner are unequally dedicated, but you will also struggle to keep your motivation. If you question their commitment, walk away from the opportunity. It is always wise to have a lawyer draw up a legally binding agreement that details the specifics of the partnership operation and dissolvent.
- **DIFFERENCE IN VALUES.** Amos 3:3 asks, *"Can two walk together, unless they are agreed?"* Unless partners are united in their values, there will be problems. Here's a hint: if you can't agree before you enter a partnership, nothing will change for the better afterward. Prevention

101 says don't jump into an agreement where agreement is lacking. It's like jumping into an alligator swamp and expecting to swim trouble-free to the other side.

- **AGREE ON THE BUSINESS PLAN.** One of the first things I learned about business is the business plan. A good plan will act as a roadmap that will guide you through each stage of starting and managing your business. Ensure your prospective partner agrees with your business plan to reduce roadside blowouts. As well as ensure that the agreement is signed. This agreement should be part of the legal document addressed earlier.

- **50/50?** Equal partnership sounds wonderful until there is a difference in opinion. At that point, whose vote carries the greater weight? Within your legal document, determine ownership percentages, power, and authority. If you choose an equal partnership, establish how to solve differences in opinions within the document. Consider an agreed-upon board of directors or board of advisors as a possible solution. Either way, ensure it's outlined in your legally binding agreement.

- **FAMILY AND FRIENDS.** When you consider that many partnerships do not survive, entering into these business relationships with people you love brings its own additional dangers. If they work, it's excellent, but if they fail, you risk straining or losing the relationship with two people at once: your business partner and your loved one. Give your decision a double dose of consideration.

I do not intend to discourage you from seeking a business partner; there are many advantages. It is my desire, however, to caution you from entering a business partnership wearing blinders and not being fully informed. Caveat emptor: let the buyer beware.

It is rare to find a business partner who is selfless. If you are lucky it happens once in a lifetime. ~ Michael Eisner

Now It's Time To Invest

Consider your personality. What would be your biggest challenge with a business partner?

What would be your greatest challenge in partnering with a family member in business?

Beyond financial, what are the advantages of a business partner?

Proactive Leadership

Have you ever met a person who always seemed to be in a crisis? They run from situation to situation in what appears to be a never-ending cycle, like a hamster on a wheel. They are continually in response mode. Some days are like that for every leader; it's impossible to anticipate every circumstance. Unexpected situations catch you off guard, and you must react at that moment; there is no time for a session to plan the solution. You analyze the situation, design the solution, and act in one breath. On days like that, after the crisis, I'm tired and need to sit back to regroup. While I'm the queen of spontaneity, I cannot imagine being a leader who constantly responds and never plans. The most incredible level of success demands proactive leadership.

Proactive leaders think long-term; they are organized in their thought processes, and their approach brings calm confidence to the team they lead. They anticipate needs and challenges, preparing themselves and the team to overcome them. They take advance control of situations by planning and preparing to avoid unnecessary challenges. When faced with a problem that requires immediate attention, the proactive leader reacts but walks away with lessons learned for organizational improvement.

On the other hand, reactive leaders wait for problems to occur before addressing them. As they move from fire to fire, there is no gathering of lessons for improving the operation or how they operate. Reactive leadership negatively affects the entire team and the organization's productivity. They eliminate the planning opportunities of others as "right now needs" preempt planned preparation. The constant preempting of plans leads to frustration within the team and a loss of job satisfaction. Ultimately, team members begin to assume a "why plan" mentality.

Leaders who want to make a lasting positive impact within their organization must set an example of proactive leadership. The focus of proactive leadership is easily divided into three areas: planning, organizing, and communicating.

Plan

- Establish priorities and plan ways to devote more time to the priorities. Don't allow distractions to pull you off task as much as possible. Most distractions can wait; plan to address them later.
- Focus on things you can control. Don't waste time pondering regrets and disappointments; learn and move forward.

- Be realistic with your time. If you have no time for planning, maybe your day is too packed. Evaluate your schedule and tasks in line with your goals. Where you can delegate, do so; where you can realign, do so; free the time to do what you must for the organization's health as a proactive leader.

Organize

- Lists provide structure and give you a sense of accomplishment. I love looking at a sheet of paper with everything lined off as I work through the priorities I've set. Armed with my list, I quickly get back on task even when the world distracts me.
- Put you on your calendar. When considering your availability, it's easy to forget your planning time if you don't schedule it. Also, plan your breaks and exercise times to keep you from burning out.
- Systems are the best friend of a proactive leader. The best system for you is the one that works best.

Communicate

- Reply quickly to notes, emails, text messages, and such. Your willingness to respond quickly allows others to be proactive leaders.

- Collaboration makes it easier to be proactive. Use meeting and task management apps to keep everyone informed and part of the planning process.
- Encouraging frequent and constructive feedback is an excellent way to stay coordinated. Respectful conversations and active listening will help team members to develop shared values and goals.

Proactive leadership is one of the most effective keys to great success. I choose to be proactive for myself, my organization, and my staff. What about you?

I believe that everyone chooses how to approach life. If you're proactive, you focus on preparing. If you're reactive, you end up focusing on repairing. ~ John C. Maxwell

Now It's Time To Invest

Are you a proactive leader or a reactive leader?

What can you do to become more proactive?

Write your thoughts about the following characteristics of a proactive leader. Include how you stack up in these areas.

- *Long-term thinker*

- *Organized*

- *Calm demeanor*

Now That I'm Ready to Win

Let me tell you something about myself. I believe in dressing for success no matter where I'm going. Now let me clarify, dressing for success doesn't mean I always wear a suit and heels. I can wear a sweatsuit, and I'm a fashion statement by the time I finish adding my personalized touches. Seriously, I receive as many compliments on my casual wear as on my formal wear. Here is my secret: once I'm entirely dressed, hair, make-up, accessories, and all, I take that final quick look in the mirror before I step out of the room. If the woman who looks back doesn't inspire me, I must figure out why and fix that. As a coach and entrepreneur, part of my assignment is to inspire others, and for me, it's a total package or nothing at all.

Now, take that same mentality into your role as a leader and entrepreneur. You are all suited up with information on how to do what you do and how to do it well. You have the vision, business plan, and vision board; you are making boss moves, building your team, taking care of yourself and your family, managing your resources, and walking tall in your purpose. You are now ready to win! However, before you step out of the room, I want you to take that final quick look in the mirror. Does the woman who looks back inspire you? WAIT! Before you answer, look closer beyond what you quickly see and check out her reputation. Are you still inspired?

How is your reputation? Do people want to work with you? How do you carry yourself? How do you respond when things don't go the way you planned? How do you treat your staff? Are you known as a giver or a taker? Is your product or service excellent, but your attitude nasty? Your credit score may be over 800, but what is your creditability score? Are you respectful to all? What is your reputation? If you have a poor reputation, no matter what else you have going for you, you are not ready to win.

Your most valuable possession is your reputation, your good name. Proverbs 22:1 says, *"A good reputation is better than much wealth; high esteem is better than silver and gold."* A good reputation attracts and retains talented, committed employees and customers willing to pay more for services. Do you google businesses before going and consider the reviews you find in your decision-making process? I do, and if their reputation is poor, I choose to spend my money elsewhere. Think about it: when was the last time you said, "Yeah, I know their service is horrible, and the staff is rude, but I like the product, so I'm going back." Yeah, right, me neither. I will find the product elsewhere or learn to live without it.

So, are you ready to take a courageous step in your life as an entrepreneur? You cannot take your word concerning your reputation alone. You may think you are the best person, selling the best product, with the best attitude, but what do others think? To discover what others think, you must ask others, but before you ask, you must "prepare" yourself for the truth. By "prepare," I mean position yourself to receive their truth without arguing, justifying, or getting upset about the input.

Throughout this journal, I've talked about having those circles of safety. Offering insight as you gauge your reputation is one of the ways they can support you. I also constantly encouraged the idea of a coach; this is another opportunity for them to assist you in your growth and development as a leader and entrepreneur. It is better to discover early in your business life about your reputation before it is a Googleable question. Allow people to be honest and specific with their answers. If you already have a business, find out from your clients what brings them back and if there are areas in customer care that need improvement. If you provide services that require you to work closer to your clients, ask them more specific questions about you and your team. Contact clients who no longer use your services and discover answers from their perspectives if possible.

What do you do with the information you obtain? Well, consider this: what would you do if you discovered you had a giant hole in the wall of your store during the winter? Would it be essential to fix it? How quickly would you repair the breach? Why would you respond immediately? Let me share my answers. It would become my #1 priority to fix the hole. I would turn all efforts and resources right there, focused on fixing that problem. It would require my immediate attention for several reasons. Resources would be lost: staff and customers, finances of earned income, and increased heating bill. It's a health and safety hazard, and the list goes on. That's the same priority you should give to issues that affect your reputation.

Monitoring, protecting, and maintaining your reputation is not a one-time evaluation. It should be a continual process. I recently celebrated 30 years as an entrepreneur. In evaluating myself, businesses, the leadership team, staff, business connections, practices, customer approach, services, and more, I found "holes in the wall." I discovered since the last time I performed a deep dive evaluation, I had changed: my approach, passion, and direction had changed. My rooms, thoughts, authority, how I speak, and my prayers had changed. I have gathered more experience and learned new things, and my vision has expanded and grown. However, I've not diligently led my teams into that change. I have not tuned into why we've experienced client and staff shifts, and I've permitted small practices that don't represent me well to continue. It was time to shift.

How does a person repair a reputation? I will tell you that it's an intentional process that takes time but is worth the work. Apologize when you need to, improve your product or services where you need to, and get help when required. Have you ever heard the saying "speed of the leader"? If you discover you need to work on your reputation because of your negative attitude, check the attitude of your staff; they often take on some of the leadership characteristics. Socrates said, *"The way to gain a good reputation is to endeavor to be what you desire to appear."* If you discover your business is suffering and limited in growth by staff members' negative attitudes and behaviors, they must be retrained, repositioned, or removed.

The benefits of a good reputation make the journey of keeping or repairing one worth the work. You have come too far to turn around; you have this!

*A brand is what a business does; reputation
is what people remember.* ~ Ted Rubin

Now It's Time To Invest

Consider three of the most common obstacles to building a rock-solid, effective business team: vague goals, lack of trust, and ineffective communication. Brainstorm below how to overcome these obstacles. If you want to step your brainstorming session up a notch, invite a few business associates or team members to join you.

Boss or Leader?

I've been an entrepreneur for most of my adult life, so my experience working for someone else is limited. I have, however, had enough experience to know the difference between a boss and a leader, and that difference, I have discovered, makes the difference in business.

Do you consider yourself a leader or a boss? This question doesn't just apply to the workplace. Consider that question honestly before you respond. Many believe the words are synonymous; however, they are opposites at their core and heart. In a world full of bosses, there are far too few leaders.

Since leaders are relatively scarce, you can make a name for yourself by becoming a good leader. The benefits experienced by a leader over a boss are many. They include increased success, fewer challenges with employees, greater job satisfaction, and a more pleasant work environment, promoting better health for everyone.

Here are a few comparisons and ideas to assist you in becoming a more successful and effective leader.

- **LEAD BY EXAMPLE.** A boss likes to sit on the sidelines and allow others to work hard. A leader is out in front of their people, showing the way. A leader is involved. A boss drops the plan and walks away.

- **LEADERS ARE DRIVEN BY A PURPOSE.** When there is an overall goal or mission, the people following the leader are inspired and empowered. They understand the assignment because the leader desires buy-in. Those sticking with the boss work from a things-to-do list without much context. Their opinion and buy-in are less critical than completing the assigned task.

- **LEADERS DELEGATE.** Leaders trust their people, but a boss, prone to micromanaging, struggles to relinquish control. A leader surrounds themselves with people who are strong in their areas of weakness. A boss hires people that don't make them feel threatened.

- **A BOSS ALWAYS HAS A WEAKER TEAM.** The boss's team can't accomplish as much because they're not empowered. The team is typically weaker because the boss doesn't want strong employees who might shine brighter than they do.

- **LEADERS VALUE RESPECT.** A leader will use his enthusiasm, skill, and expertise to encourage others to respect and follow him. A boss wants to be feared and will use fear and threats to gain compliance. On the surface, they might appear to be similar, but the differences are striking.

- **A LEADER DEVELOPS NEW LEADERS.** A true leader constantly creates employees with the knowledge and experience to take their place. A boss is afraid of competition. A boss is worried about being replaced and is too self-centered to be concerned about the career aspirations of others.

- **LEADERS KNOW HOW TO MOTIVATE.** Leaders know that no two employees are the same. They invest time in getting to know their employees well enough to know how to inspire them. The mentality of a boss says, "It is what it is. This is what needs to be done. You can always look for another job if you don't like it."
- **LEADERS USE POSITIVE TECHNIQUES FOR MOTIVATION.** Leaders look for ways to encourage and motivate the team. In comparison, bosses tend to use criticism as a motivational tool. After all, who wants to be called out and embarrassed?
- **LEADERS TAKE RESPONSIBILITY.** When the team fails, the leader is in front, taking the brunt of the criticism. When the crew of a boss fails, the boss tries to absolve himself of as much responsibility as possible. While a boss is quick to blame his employees, a leader is quick to blame himself.

Think back over your work history. You've probably had plenty of bosses and, hopefully, at least a few leaders. Working for someone who fits into the boss category is not enjoyable. You feel like you're operating in the dark with little support and few development opportunities. Especially in this age of employees putting job satisfaction higher on their list of what is essential in a workplace, the organization led by a boss will find that quality team members will move on quickly.

Develop your leadership skills. It's much more enjoyable and beneficial to work for a leader. You'll be helping yourself, your employees, your organization, and your family. Be the leader you dreamed of leading you into great success.

People ask the difference between a leader and a boss. The leader leads, and the boss drives." ~ Theodore Roosevelt.

Now It's Time To Invest

Read Proverbs 22:1 (CBE). Discuss the meaning of this Scripture.

Do you lead people or tell them what you want them to do without consideration or explanation? What effect does this style of management have on a team? Do you encourage and develop your team or use criticism to protect your interests? Gather a few friends to discuss the questions and answers.

Are you a leader with a few boss ways? What are you willing to do to alter your practices if those ways are not conducive to victory in your organization? Identify the ways and what you plan to do to change.

Entrepreneurship Doesn't Mean Leave Your 9-5

As entrepreneurs, we make many decisions every day. Some will be simple and clear-cut, not requiring much time and energy investment. However, other choices before us will leave us staring at the ceiling at midnight as the information gathered, possibilities investigated, and counsel received rumbles around in our heads. For many entrepreneurs, one of those challenging times will occur when deciding if and when to leave full-time employment to pursue their passion.

The good thing, which is also the challenging thing about this decision, is that there is no absolute answer to fit every entrepreneur. The choice depends on so many unique factors it is impossible to say what is right or wrong for every person. There are compelling testimonies of people who jumped right into their business and zoomed to the top. There are also stories of others who seemed to have everything lined up to make the transition, and the business failure caused them to return to a 9-5.

My story — I started as an entrepreneur and never looked back. While I've considered some drastic downsizing during exceptionally tough seasons, entering a 9-5 type situation has never appealed to me. Some people have never taken their side hustle to a full-time business, while others go full-time in their entrepreneurial endeavors and keep a traditional part-time position. In the business of business, there are no guarantees, and you cannot determine the right time to launch like a mathematical equation. The bottom line is what is right or wrong for you; it's your choice. However, there are areas to look at and situations to consider in your decision-making process.

My purpose is to provide you with areas to consider and research further as you consider your next step as an entrepreneur. I wouldn't dare attempt to mention everything you should consider in deciding when and if to leave your job to pursue your passion; that would require volumes and still only scratch the surface. You know I'm transparent; I never want to give the illusion that I made all the right choices. The truth is that I missed the mark many times and faced the unpleasant consequences of my selections. That's part of why I'm so passionate about coaching. I go hard to help as many as possible, not feel alone while allowing them to reap the benefits from my experience.

Let's look at five areas that warrant your consideration and preparation.

1. **FINANCES.** Look at your finances realistically. How much startup capital do you need? How long until you can break even and earn a

profit? How much money do you currently need to keep living? Do you have others who depend on your income? If so, how will your decision affect them? What benefits does your current position offer that you will be responsible for if you resign, like medical insurance? How much of a cash cushion do you need?

2. **MARKET.** What is the current demand for your product or service? Do you have enough team and resources to shoulder the demand for more? Whatever you sell now, you will have to produce and sell more. To offer your service on a larger scale, will you need to hire more people immediately?

3. **VERIFIED PLAN.** Invest the time to test and verify the business model for your product or service. You may think they are the best cookies in the world, and they may be good, the hit of the family gathering, but if you plan to sell them for double the current selling price, you might want to test that plan before leaving your 9-5.

4. **PLAN THE PLAN.** Starting a new adventure as your own boss may sound exciting, and it is, but the joy dwindles when you don't make money. You will still have financial obligations. Plan and prepare in ways to be more frugal. How will you use the extra time once you resign from your full-time position? Plan how your day will go. Get a planner or a project management app and begin to plan. Both will help you stay on track as you pursue your passion fully.

5. **ARE YOU READY?** Are you ready to thrive under the pressure of an entrepreneur's everyday life? Are you ready to pour yourself into your side hustle? Are you emotionally ready to learn new things and create contacts as you involve yourself in the typical day-to-day challenges

of an entrepreneur? Are you ready for long hours? How's your health? Are any surgeries planned? How are your children? Are any of your children entering college? A decision to leave your full-time position to turn your side hustle into a thriving business will touch every area of your life; ensure you are ready.

After considering all that and more, talking to fellow entrepreneurs and coaches, praying, and lining up all your resources and support, remember the choice is yours, as are the consequences. Move forward when the time is right for you.

When you have a dream, you've got to grab
it and never let go. ~ Carol Burnett

Now It's Time To Invest

Sponsor a brainstorming session this week. Invite a couple of people you know with a side hustle and a full-time job. Discuss the idea of leaving your job to embrace your passion fully. Share ideas, fears, plans, and possibilities. In a room of people of like minds, gather wisdom. Even if you are not ready right now, save it for the future. You could put some of your findings here, but I suggest you get a notebook, journal, or, in a section of your phone, start a WHEN I'M READY book. Keep it handy and add as you go. The gathered information will be priceless when the time is right.

Wealth — Not Just About $

Some people exclusively equate financial success with wealth. Having enough money is a part of wealth, but there's much more to it. Is obtaining money, profit, and financial abundance number one on your list in building success? Take a moment and answer these questions for me.

What's more important to you?

A. Close family ties	B. Millions in the bank
A. Your good health	B. Large savings
A. Peace in your heart	B. A fat 401k
A. Strong marriage	B. A mansion
A. Great relationship with kids	B. Massive profits
A. Talk to a loved one you miss	B. Win the lotto
A. Profiting mind	B. Profiting investments
A. Knowing you are loved	B. Knowing your banker

For most people, your answers are A across the board. That said, we can agree that money, financial wealth, and all money can buy are not essential to wealthy living. I'm amazed and saddened by the number of people who take their lives, and that number includes very rich people.

Don't misunderstand my intent; there is nothing wrong with money, profit, and enjoying the things finances can buy. I love the benefits and opportunities offered to our family because of the businesses, financial planning, and preparation of Steve and myself. My point is that the wallet is not where wealth stops.

As you pursue success and wealth, let me encourage you to pursue at the same level in every area of your life. As you invest in the stock market, don't forget to invest in your family, marriage, health, staff members, education, etc. It's easy to get caught up in hustling for the next deal, sale, or accomplishment while forgetting to invest in what is most important.

Money does solve some challenges, but not all. As you face challenges, resist the urge to think all your problems will go away with more money and the way to make more money is to work more, hustle harder, invest more time in the grind, and be away from life. While seeing that profit bar rise may excite you momentarily, the thrill will depart when another financial crisis occurs. On the other hand, investing time with your children at an amusement park or attending one of their games will give you both a return on your investment that will last a lifetime. Avoid the temptation to make a living at the expense of making a life.

Do things to keep yourself healthy: exercise, eat right, sleep, and resist excessive stress. You will not be wealthy in your health if you allow pressure to reign freely within your mind and body. Invest in yourself, your education, your marriage, and your friendships. If you don't intentionally balance your life, it will suffer while your pockets get fatter.

While we do not always get it right, Steve and I work hard to keep a balanced life where our priorities are clearly defined. It's not easy, but it's possible and vital. The most important things in life are valuable, but they are not for sale! Remember to invest in all areas.

A real measure of your wealth is how much you would be worth if you lost all of your money. ~ Unknown

Now It's Time To Invest

List the five most important things in your life. Now, think about the time you have invested into each of them over the past week. Are you balanced? Or do you need to do some adjusting?

Think of ways to increase your investment in areas of your life that need more of your attention.

Which part of your life is the most satisfying? Why?

Thank You

Some behaviors and mindsets that stick with me even today were taught to me growing up. In some cases, I don't remember an adult sitting down and instructing me, but I will never forget them living the example before me. One of those mindsets is gratitude. I'm a grateful woman! I am very thankful. I appreciate all God has done in my life — my health, family, "framily" (friends who became family), friends, ministry, businesses, associates, and opportunities; I could go on forever.

I have discovered that gratitude is a natural part of my life that spills over into every area of my world. Expressing my appreciation to people is a genuine part of who I am. It's imperative to me that people know how much I value them and their presence in my life. I don't have to write a list of people I want to thank; my heart is filled with them.

One of the most potent phrases in any language is "thank you." With those words, you have the power to make someone's day. It's crazy how, at a checkout counter, an earnest "Thank you. Have a great day." given with a smile changes the countenance of the cashier. If a simple thank you has that effect on a stranger, think of the impact an expression of gratitude has on someone you know.

Yes, someone you know. Don't ever think that because you know them, love them, live with them, they work for you, or they're your children, they don't need to hear thank you or other expressions of gratitude. As William Arthur Ward said, *"Feeling gratitude and not expressing it is like wrapping a present and not giving it."* I desire to express my gratitude to everyone, especially those closest to me. I read somewhere that when you take things for granted the things you are granted get taken. I never want to take anyone for granted. I would never want to lose or lessen the value of the relationships and people in my life. It's important to me that people know how grateful I am for them and their presence in my world.

Loyalty is not for sale; it can only be earned, and expressions of gratitude are investments that lead to a loyal team. I have seen business owners who say they value their staff but don't invest in showing what they say. Loosen the grip on your wallet; while your investment can and at times should call for your finances to be involved, every act of gratitude should not affect your wallet.

Here are a few simple ideas that say thank you.

- **SMILE.** Show your appreciation with a smile; it's easy and only costs $free.99.

- **SEND A NOTE.** Text, email, post on social media, or send a card in the mail. I know a picture is worth a thousand words, but a few words of gratitude are worth more than a picture.

- **A SPECIAL GIFT.** Think out of the box; it doesn't have to break your budget. If you're out and see something that screams their name, grab it. An annual subscription to PURE FLIX or a favorite magazine, a cup of coffee and a favorite pastry, a gift certificate, or delivered chocolate-covered strawberries are great ways to say thank you.

- **COFFEE FOR 2.** Invite them for coffee, breakfast, lunch, or dinner. The time or place is not as important as the purpose.

- **BRAG.** When the opportunity presents itself, brag on them. You let them and others know how much you appreciate them.

- **PERSONAL TOUCH.** Say thank you with a homemade gift, a batch of homemade cookies, or another yummy treat you know they will appreciate. Let me help you; just because I say "homemade" doesn't mean you must make it in your home. If you're like me, multitalented but homemade is not my favorite lane. Find a local who does that kind of thing. It's a win for everyone; a fellow entrepreneur receives business, someone is shown gratitude and loves the gift, and I can answer to the passion of my heart by expressing gratitude!

- **PHONE CALL.** Sometimes, a simple phone call is all you need to communicate how you appreciate someone. If they don't answer, leave a message that shares your gratefulness.

The only limit is your imagination. If you go the extra mile to show someone you're genuinely grateful, they will remember the gesture for a long time. Take the time and invest regularly; discover 100 ways to say thank you.

Living in a state of gratitude is the gateway
to grace. ~ Arianna Huffington

Now It's Time To Invest

Strengthen a significant relationship in your life today. Choose one of these ideas or come up with your own and say "thank you" to someone special meaningfully.

Do you say thank you to others often enough? Do you express gratitude routinely to those in your life? If not, what will you do to correct that?

How do you feel when others do not express their appreciation for you?

Give Yourself Grace

If you've invested a week with every journal topic, you have reached 1-year in this journey! I bet you have grown as you have applied yourself, celebrated the victories, and rolled around on the floor, kicking your feet (on the inside, of course) in the struggles. The person reading this is not the same person who read the first journal topic 52 weeks ago. Let me be the 2nd person to congratulate you on a job well done; the 1st person should have been yourself.

As you look back over the year behind you, I ask that you do so with one word at the forefront of your thinking: *grace*. This journal's first and last topics are the same: *Give Yourself Grace*. The topic is identical because I believe that often, we are so hard on ourselves as we consider what we accomplished well and where we need to grow. You have learned a lot this year. Indeed, you didn't make all the right choices, nor did I. In some instances, you moved too slowly, and so did I. When presented with other opportunities, you moved too quickly and lived to regret it; hey, me too! This year, you lost your temper when you should have closed your mouth; girl, move over. I'm in this boat, too. Some prospects you blew, and there is no chance of a redo; I got the t-shirt; what size you wear, I'll grab you one too. What am I saying? Grace on you! Grace on me!

As an entrepreneur, wife, mother, pastor, friend, and sister, I have grown to understand the saying, *"No sense in crying over spilled milk."* I clean it up, learn from it, and move forward; I encourage you to do the same. Some people may misinterpret your disposition of grace as nonchalant or indifferent. When you can, help them understand; it's grace.

Celebrate your victories from the past year. Get your family and support circle to join you in the celebration. Gather the lessons learned from the moments and opportunities that did not go so well. Celebrate that you survived, learned, and thrived through it all! Celebrate those still standing with you and those who are no longer there. Celebrate the lives you touched and those who touched your life. Celebrate the people who hurt you. The encounter made you stronger and taught you much; did you learn? Celebrate the person you were and the person you have become. Celebrate grace.

You did it! You discovered the next level within you and stepped up like a boss!

> *It's ok not to have it all together all the time.*
> *Give yourself grace.* ~ Unknown

Now It's Time To Invest

Look at the photograph of me on the front cover. Now, take a look at the picture of me on the back cover. In August 2022, I weighed 244 pounds (front cover); the back photo is my most recent, taken in October 2023 and 54 pounds later. With consistent determination, I applied principles, some of which I have shared in this journal, to my weight loss desires. I challenge you to apply yourself to what I've shared here, and you too will begin to lose the weight that weighs you down preventing you from stepping into your next level. Don't quit! Now, what is the one obstacle that just popped into your head? Write it down. What are you going to do?

Before you begin your celebration, list your accomplishments, large and small, over the last year. You will need extra sheets of paper.

Let's get going; it's celebration time! Plan your celebration. Where will you go, what will you do, and who is on the guest list to attend?

After setting the plans for the celebration, before the fiesta begins, think about what's next. Start writing.

The Circle that Surrounds You

*Treat people better than you would treat yourself. Exceed
their expectations every time.* ~ Nicole L. Brown

*Real men treat the janitor with the same
respect as the CEO.* ~ Michelle Obama

*Don't be afraid to sit in rooms you have been invited
to join. You belong there.* ~ Nicole L. Brown

*No one can whistle a symphony. It takes a whole
orchestra to play it.* ~ H. E. Luccock

*Alone we can do so little; together we
can do so much.* ~ Helen Keller

Let go when it's time to let go. ~ Nicole L. Brown

*Don't let pride stand in your way of your success. Even
Michael Jordan had a coach.* ~ Shanel Evans, Friend

You are not alone! ~ Nicole L. Brown

Friendships between women, as any woman will tell you, are built of a thousand small kindnesses... swapped back and forth and over again. ~ Michelle Obama

My why is greater than my fear! ~ Nicole L. Brown

When you're different, sometimes you don't see the millions of people who accept you for what you are. All you notice is the person who doesn't. ~ Jodi Picoult

IT IS POSSIBLE! ~ Nicole L. Brown

About the Author

Nicole L. Brown is a woman of many gifts and talents. She uses all of them to encourage others to push past internal and external obstacles to become the greatest possible version of themselves. She is an entrepreneur's entrepreneur with more than 30 years of experience.

Nicole began with an in-home daycare licensed for 12 children, and now she is the owner and CEO of Nikki's Christian Learning Center with three sites in Virginia. Her love for fashion and desire to help others realize you can look amazing within your budget led her to open Nikki B. Jewels, a fashion boutique home based in one of Virginia's most prestigious malls. Her passion for seeing others succeed led her to formally step into the world of entrepreneur coaching. Her open and passionate way of communicating captures the hearts of listeners and has created a demand for her as a motivational speaker. Her love for God, His Word, and His people continues to unlock doors of opportunities for this amazing woman within circles of power and influence.

Nicole L. Brown and her husband, Stephen L. Brown, serve together as Pastors of Life Connect Community Church, an explosive ministry in Woodbridge, Virginia. They have had the honor of raising four amazing children, each of which are creating marks of greatness in their own right: one son, two daughters, and a godson: Stephen, Nikki, Stephanie, and Ricky. Added to Team Brown are two bonus daughters, Rhema Joy and Tyler.

www.ingramcontent.com/pod-product-compliance
Lightning Source LLC
Chambersburg PA
CBHW081325120626
46546CB00011B/3217